PowerGen is delighted
to join the nation in congratulating
Her Majesty The Queen
on the 40th anniversary of her accession.

PowerGen generating electricity
now and for future generations.

GEC IS PROUD TO SHARE IN THE

CELEBRATION OF THE 40TH

ANNIVERSARY OF HER MAJESTY

QUEEN ELIZABETH II's ACCESSION.

GEC COMPANIES HAVE BEEN

PROUD WINNERS OF MANY

QUEEN'S AWARDS FOR EXPORTS AND

TECHNOLOGICAL ACHIEVEMENTS.

The General Electric Company, p.l.c.

H.M. Queen Elizabeth II
A Celebration of Forty Years

❖
❖

PUBLISHED BY
Atalink Ltd.
40 Bowling Green Lane
London EC1R 0NE
Telephone: 071-837 6136
Under licence from Celebration 1992 Ltd.

LICENSEES
Atalink Ltd. and RPC, The Regency Press Corporation Ltd.

CONCEIVED BY
Richard Kyle

PUBLISHER
Charles Gregoriou

CONTRIBUTING EDITOR
Godfrey Talbot LVO, OBE

EDITOR
Joyce Quarrie

PICTURE EDITOR
Millie Simpson

LAYOUT, DESIGN & TYPESETTING
Mike Lamb
Goldencroft Ltd., Bromley, Kent

COVER DESIGN
Leyland Gomez

PRODUCTION SUPPORT
Nancy Clarke, Sally Hooker, Nadine van Overstraeten

PUBLIC RELATIONS CONSULTANT
Sonia Seymour-Williams

PROJECT MANAGEMENT
R&P Consultants t/a
RPC Advertising & Public Relations
Gordon House, 6 Lissenden Gardens
London NW5 1LX
Telephone: 071-485 9351

PROJECT MANAGER
Jane Gee

MARKETING
Richard Ansell, Robert Bache, Kevin Barry,
Stephen Fenton, David Hancock, Clive Hunter-Dunne, Lena Manning,
David O'Brien, Brian Parrish, Richard Verden

REPRODUCTION
CCF Repro Services
London E9 5BL

PRINTED BY
Passmore International
Maidstone

PAPER SUPPLIED BY
Robert Horne Paper Co. Ltd.
London

DISTRIBUTED BY
SM Magazine Distribution Ltd.
London

HER MAJESTY THE QUEEN'S
40TH ANNIVERSARY

*L*ittlewoods Pools
are delighted to extend
their warmest good wishes
and congratulations to
Her Majesty the Queen

LITTLEWOODS POOLS

CONTENTS

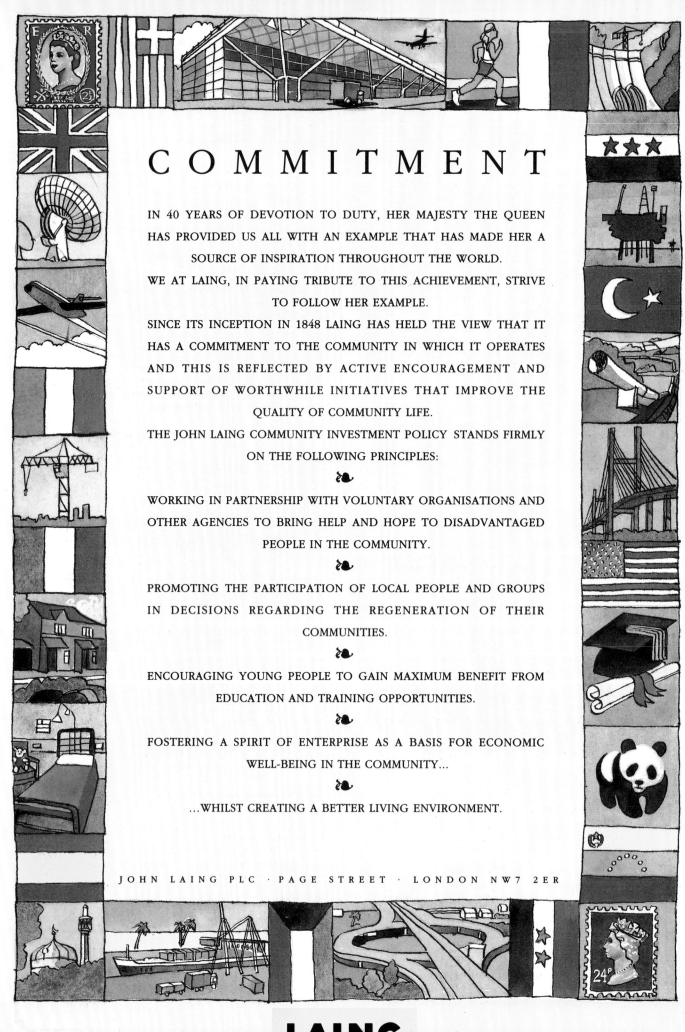

COMMITMENT

IN 40 YEARS OF DEVOTION TO DUTY, HER MAJESTY THE QUEEN HAS PROVIDED US ALL WITH AN EXAMPLE THAT HAS MADE HER A SOURCE OF INSPIRATION THROUGHOUT THE WORLD.

WE AT LAING, IN PAYING TRIBUTE TO THIS ACHIEVEMENT, STRIVE TO FOLLOW HER EXAMPLE.

SINCE ITS INCEPTION IN 1848 LAING HAS HELD THE VIEW THAT IT HAS A COMMITMENT TO THE COMMUNITY IN WHICH IT OPERATES AND THIS IS REFLECTED BY ACTIVE ENCOURAGEMENT AND SUPPORT OF WORTHWHILE INITIATIVES THAT IMPROVE THE QUALITY OF COMMUNITY LIFE.

THE JOHN LAING COMMUNITY INVESTMENT POLICY STANDS FIRMLY ON THE FOLLOWING PRINCIPLES:

WORKING IN PARTNERSHIP WITH VOLUNTARY ORGANISATIONS AND OTHER AGENCIES TO BRING HELP AND HOPE TO DISADVANTAGED PEOPLE IN THE COMMUNITY.

PROMOTING THE PARTICIPATION OF LOCAL PEOPLE AND GROUPS IN DECISIONS REGARDING THE REGENERATION OF THEIR COMMUNITIES.

ENCOURAGING YOUNG PEOPLE TO GAIN MAXIMUM BENEFIT FROM EDUCATION AND TRAINING OPPORTUNITIES.

FOSTERING A SPIRIT OF ENTERPRISE AS A BASIS FOR ECONOMIC WELL-BEING IN THE COMMUNITY...

...WHILST CREATING A BETTER LIVING ENVIRONMENT.

JOHN LAING PLC · PAGE STREET · LONDON NW7 2ER

LAING

CONSTRUCTION WORLDWIDE

CONTENTS

THE BOC GROUP

FOREWORD

❖
_____
❖

*F*or forty years the firm identity of Her Majesty Queen Elizabeth II has been unmistakably stamped upon the decades, memories of which are recalled in this publication.

It is a kaleidoscope of salutes from specialist writers, and from the business world, all wishing to pay homage to one of the longest serving monarchs alive today. But it would be wrong to believe that any of these salutes were the result of a 'Royal Command'. What Her Majesty has done is simply given her approval to the setting up of a nationwide programme of events throughout 1992, focusing on educational and social benefits rather than pageantry, under the auspices of a new charitable organisation, The Royal Anniversary Trust.

This book is a souvenir of the anniversary, a celebration of forty years, and a salute to the steadfast and stalwart qualities which Her Majesty has displayed in her devotion to duty. It acts as an expression in words and pictures of the thanks of millions of people for her service to the nation, the Commonwealth and the world.

We all have many reasons to be grateful for the way in which Queen Elizabeth II has committed herself totally to serving her people and to join together in saying Long Live The Queen.

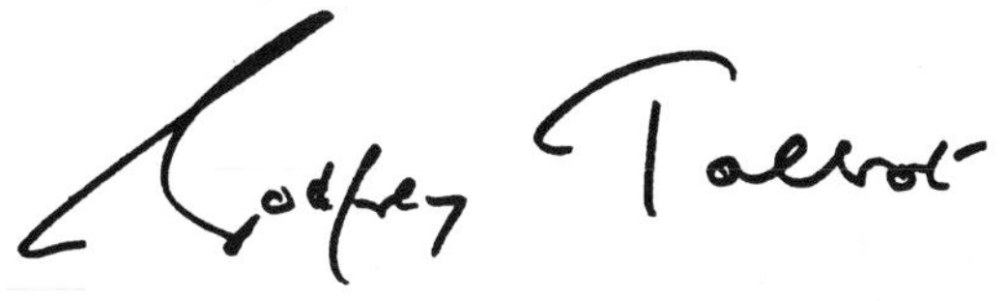

Godfrey Talbot

You talk. We listen.

And together we'll build the future.

You need a special kind of vision to run your business successfully.

To see ahead and plan for tomorrow.

You need a special kind of vision to make sure you're always one step ahead of your competitors.

To capitalise on opportunities. Wherever they occur in the world.

And communications are simply too vital to entrust to anyone that doesn't share such an outlook with you.

But we do.

BT is one of the world's leading communications companies. We are totally committed to understanding how people and businesses can communicate effectively.

For it is only when we have listened to your needs that we can respond with the most powerful solution.

We understand business. We understand communications.

Together we can be a formidable force.

THE ROYAL ANNIVERSARY TRUST

In July 1990, The Royal Anniversary Trust — a charity — was established under the chairmanship of the Rt. Hon. George Younger MP with a distinguished panel of trustees, organising a programme of celebrations for the 40th anniversary of the Queen's accession to the throne on 6 February 1952. The project, which was initiated and developed by Robin Gill, a trustee and Chairman of the Organisation and Executive, has been supported by John Major, the Prime Minister, Neil Kinnock and Paddy Ashdown and is approved by Buckingham Palace. The principal financial support is derived from industry and commerce throughout the United Kingdom. No government funds are involved.

There are four major programmes in the celebrations during 1992. The Sovereign Exhibition at the Victoria & Albert Museum, London from 3 April to 13 September, portrays in artifacts, many of which have not previously been seen by the public, the working life and responsibilities of the Queen. The curator of the exhibition is Lord Norwich and it is designed by the Royal College of Art (Design) Ltd. The sponsors are Pearson, Reed International and The Daily Telegraph.

Sections will include "Pomp and Circumstance", capturing the majesty of royal occasions with a dazzling array of decorations and costumes . . . "The Queen and Commonwealth", illustrating the Queen's role on the world stage . . . and "The Monarch and the Media", examining the Queen's evolving relationship with the press, TV and radio.

The Schools Awards Programme offers an exciting opportunity for young people in the nation's schools and colleges to work together in devising and executing imaginative projects of lasting benefit to their communities, environment, particularly outside their schools.

Adults can also play their part in expressing their gratitude to the Queen through The Royal Anniversary Challenge. This invites groups, associations, clubs and individuals to make proposals for activities that will be of lasting benefit to the young, the elderly or those with special needs.

National Awards ceremonies for both The Schools Awards Programme and The Royal Anniversary Challenge are expected to be held in the late autumn.

The programme of celebrations culminates on 26 October with a gala spectacular at Earls Court Arena II which will be televised by the BBC and transmitted abroad. It will depict Britain's achievements in the 40 years of Her Majesty's reign, and contains a special tribute to the Queen when she will be presented with The Commonwealth Mace.

I take this opportunity on behalf of myself and of my colleagues worldwide at Samsung Electronics Co., Ltd. to convey our congratulations on the occasion of the Fortieth Anniversary of Her Majesty's Accession.

It is with greatest admiration and respect for her guidance, encompassing the solid principles of co-operation with world responsibility which crosses all borders, that we send our sincere gratitude for the hope and inspiration that her example has provided to us all.

As one of the world's leading industrial organizations, it is under our corporate slogan "Technology that Works for Life", that we are helping to create a better world through environmentally responsible policies for all our global activities. In assuming as wide a span of influence and provision as possible, we aim to promote a common belief to all.

As a Korean Flagship, it is to the United Kingdom that we look as being one of the countries of progression within the European Community. It is there that we have placed our lead investments in order that we too may participate in Europe's future. With the timely advent of full European co-operation, which is beneficial to causes reaching far beyond those of a purely commercial nature, and the Fortieth Anniversary of Queen Elizabeth II's accession, may her example become an integral part of the early initiatives of the European Community.

May Her Majesty long remain in good health and her contribution as a world figurehead to the welfare of the human race be with us for many more years to come.

Jin Ku Kang

Jin-Ku Kang
Chairman & C.E.O.

Technology that works for life.

20th Floor Joong-Ang Daily News Building 7, Soonwha-Dong, Chung-Ku, C.P.O. Box 2775 Seoul, Korea Cable Address. Elekstar Seoul
Telex: K27364, K23471 Samsan Telephone: (02) 751-6114 Telefax: (02) 751-6969

THE 40TH ANNIVERSARY PROGRAMME

The core programme for the 40th Anniversary celebrations has deliberately been made as flexible and wide-ranging as possible. The aim of the Royal Anniversary Trust has been to ensure that everyone can participate, but people throughout the country can express their support in their own way.

Several core themes form a common thread integrating the Trust's events.

Lasting benefit is the central theme of the Trust's challenge to groups and individuals throughout the country. The schools and adult programmes have been designed to ensure that, in years to come, communities will still be enjoying the fruits of projects undertaken in 1992 to mark the anniversary. This forward-looking aspect of the celebrations has also been reflected in the Trust's strong focus on young people through participation by schools.

The programme also aims to educate and inform. Projects such as the Sovereign Exhibition and televised Grand Finale will recognise the enormous achievements of the past 40 years. They will also consider the duties and activities of our head of state both within the country and in the Commonwealth, Europe and elsewhere. Here, too, 'lasting benefit' will be a central theme.

In inviting as many people as possible to take part, 'challenge' has been made another core theme. The Trust hopes to stimulate active participation in a range of projects that are both worthwhile and thoroughly enjoyable.

This official photograph by David Secombe was commissioned by The Royal Anniversary Trust.

The Sime Darby Group and

its many business associates and friends

throughout the Commonwealth and the Asean Region,

respectfully offer warm and sincere congratulations to

Her Majesty Queen Elizabeth II

on the occasion of the fortieth year of her reign as

Queen of the United Kingdom and Head of the Commonwealth.

Sime Darby is proud to follow the example set by

Her Majesty and the Royal Family

in their pursuit of excellence in the quality of community life.

In today's challenging social climate,

Her Majesty has been an inspiration to the youth of the world.

Her concern for upholding educational standards,

caring for the environment and

for a return to traditional family values is

one we at Sime Darby share with her Majesty.

We wish Her Majesty and the Commonwealth of Nations

a prosperous and secure future.

Tun Ismail bin Mohamed Ali
Chairman

Sime Darby Berhad
21st Floor, Wisma Sime Darby
Jalan Raja Laut
50350 Kuala Lumpur
Malaysia

An official Royal Anniversary Trust portrait taken to mark the fortieth anniversary of the Queen's accession.

> **"** The truest and highest form of enlightened self-interest requires that we pay the fullest regard to the interest and welfare of those around us, whose well-being we must bind up with our own... **"**
>
> **William Hesketh Lever 1900**

In the UK, Unilever's long and successful tradition of working for the well-being of the community goes back more than 100 years to William Hesketh Lever, founder of Lever Brothers and Port Sunlight Village.

He believed that good citizenship meant good business, improving the environment in which businesses operate and providing a way for the community to share in the company's commercial success.

Unilever and its operating companies continue to apply these principles today, in ways which meet current needs and make good use of our strengths. Priorities in the UK include working with schools, colleges and universities, contributing to national education projects, providing training opportunities for young people, helping small businesses to develop, supporting environmental projects, and making donations to local charities.

The pursuit of excellence is as important in community activities as it is in business. Both are approached with commitment and professionalism by Unilever's companies and employees.

Michael Angus.

Sir Michael Angus
Chairman, Unilever PLC

Unilever

A Devoted Monarch

by Godfrey Talbot, LVO, OBE

For forty years, Queen Elizabeth II has dedicated herself wholeheartedly to the role she inherited from her father on February 6, 1952. Godfrey Talbot, the most experienced royal commentator alive, looks back over the four decades of her rule as well as the years leading up to the Queen's accession.

Outlining the story of Queen Elizabeth II — and, particularly, Her Majesty's decades as Sovereign — is an engrossing exercise because her reign has seen Britain's ancient monarchy evolve and adapt and endure very notably, its routines meshed with revolutionary national and international events.

In the years we are celebrating there have probably been more changes influencing both the Sovereign Lady and ourselves than Crown and country have known in any similar period during our thousand years of kings and queens.

This Queen is the 42nd monarch since William the Conqueror. British people look on her as not only the Head of State but at the same time as an interesting human being. A meeting with her usually engenders respect for her evident experience and firmness of character which enables her never to put a foot wrong. The antithesis of a show-off herself, and not given to public exhibition of sightseers' gestures, she nevertheless leaves an impression of likeable awareness, of quiet commonsense with a quick spark of humour lurking to peep out from her composure.

Her Majesty presides with unaffected sincerity over the unity which we properly call the Family Monarchy — 'The Firm' is her husband's term for it — and by nature she pursues in that job a rare standard of excellence. She is something stable to hold on to in the maelstroms of world turmoil, for already she has ridden through wars, a dismantling of Empire and bumpy progress through the years towards a new type of association in Europe.

The Queen is solidly in position (despite tabloid press sniping at certain of her clan) because she is a firm believer in bending to duty and yet 'moving with the times'. She is an example of learning-by-experience and yet obtaining as good an education-for-good-citizenship as possible (even though her own necessarily secluded schooling during wartime was far from exciting). She did not *ask* to be Queen: the post came to her by a quirk of heredity. But once she had taken on the role she successfully reconciled her privileged position with a society which frankly favours earned wealth against inherited affluence. She has won widespread regard by being the honest and unpretentious person that she is; and ever since she came 'of age' she has, without exaggeration, devoted her life to the service of her subjects.

Hers is an inescapably public existence; and indeed, as I have said, in the public gaze she very often looks very solemn (unlike the quite natural emotional warmths which are patent in her mother, in public as in private). But that is not the whole story. Understandably, most of the public can know the Queen only 'at arm's length' and not as a private person, and thus can hardly believe that in her home and domestic life she is in fact most lively and spontaneous. Her family and personal friends know that she jokes, laughs readily, sees the funny side of things, enjoys many of the same entertainments as ordinary folk do, expresses sharp opinions, watches her weight — and television.

Her Majesty cannot, of course, ever be 'just an ordinary person' like people on the other side of palace walls. She is established as a renowned person, so everlastingly a remote world figure that it is far from easy to know the truth that essentially she is also a good wife, mother and grannie — and enjoys being those things. Indeed there is quite often something pleasantly 'ordinary' in her appearance on the less ceremonial public occasions. And perhaps she is liked for just that. If so, it is a happy thing, for her occupation may properly be described as 'representational' — that is, being all things to all people.

Hers has also often been called, quite correctly, a cushioned life, because she never has had to suffer the bus-queue kind of aggravations of ordinary folk. But at the

Princess Elizabeth photographed by her father, the then Duke of York, circa 1929.

same time she is so inexorably in the grip of duties carried out in public that her routines are by no means universally enviable. One of her Private Secretaries' memoranda to a House of Commons committee examining the Civil List (allowances to royal persons for expenses) had this passage: 'The Queen can never enjoy these engagements with the freedom of a holiday maker: the pleasure of attending them is bound to be tempered by the strain imposed on her as a public figure and by the knowledge that somebody is looking at her all the time and that she is being continually photographed. The strain of a long day taking a lively interest in everything, saying a kind word here and asking a question there, always smiling and acknowledging cheers when driving in her car, sometimes for hours, has to be experienced to be properly appreciated.'

But my business in this article is to outline the facts of the Queen's years, though perhaps bringing some of them to easy recall by personal memories.

First, there is the sheer arithmetic of Her Majesty's reign: forty years so far. Hers is already one of history's lengthy reigns: it is now only four years shorter than her Tudor namesake's famous span; and longer than the personally effective rule of George III (though nominally he was the Sovereign for over half a century). Queen Victoria of course holds the record: she occupied the Throne for 63 years. Our own Queen's grandfather, King George V, was monarch for twenty-five years. He was followed by his eldest son — the Queen's uncle — who abandoned his post within one year: he had reigned for a mere 325 days as Edward VIII when he abdicated in 1936. Then came the Queen's father, George VI, who was King for fifteen years.

An early portrait of the young Princess Elizabeth.

A Princess's Upbringing

And so to the present reign. Her Majesty was only 25 when she came to the Throne. Like her father and grandfather before her, she was not born in direct line of succession. She began life as Princess Elizabeth Alexandra Mary, first of the two children of the then Duke and Duchess of York, and she first saw the light of day — on April 21, 1926 — in the London home of her maternal grandparents, the Earl and Countess of Strathmore. The birth was scarcely front-page news, for the baby's eminent future was not envisaged. King George V, the other grandfather, was firmly on the throne, and the child's Uncle David, the Prince of Wales who was the King's heir, was fully expected to succeed in due

course — and it was reasonably expected that he would marry and have children to succeed *him*. Princess Elizabeth's father, the Duke of York, was only the monarch's *second* son. Besides, there could be reckoned every possibility that he would, later, have one or more sons who, by the rules of the Royal Line's traditional male chauvinism, would have precedence over a mere daughter — however much older she might be. Therefore, Princess Elizabeth was far enough from Sovereignty, it seemed.

But this surmised line of march to occupation of Buckingham Palace was not to happen. The Yorks produced only one further child, another daughter, Margaret in 1930; and the self-indulgent Edward VIII, infatuated by an American divorcee, deserted his whole kingly position in that 1936 sensation and went away into self-imposed exile.

That famous abdication was the turn of events which moved Princess Elizabeth close to occupation of the British throne. The throwing up of his job by Edward ('Uncle David' to Her Royal Highness) was shockingly unprecedented. It rocked the monarchy. But fortunately the mantle of sovereignty fell upon that younger brother, the Princess's father — who, shy and hesitant and understandably reluctant to take office though he was, did his constitutional duty and eventually became a respected royal leader in his own right.

A 12th birthday photograph of Princess Elizabeth out riding in Windsor Great Park with her sister and father.

The reign of George VI spanned the Second World War and was a period of great change, social and political and industrial. And the King, never physically robust, saw the hard years through with painstaking and taxing steadfastness —

Your Majesty

I am both pleased and honoured, as Chairman of the Bulgarian Committee for Tourism, to offer you my most heartfelt congratulations on the memorable occasion of your 40th Anniversary as Queen and Sovereign.

Bulgaria is a country which is small in size, but rich in natural assets - its scenery, traditions and culture offer much to the visitor - and myself and my colleagues will do our very best in the exciting new conditions made possible by the political and economic changes currently underway to enhance and improve the links between our countries, which tourism creates.

Bulgaria is truly the "Country of Roses" and I would like to make a symbolic presentation to you of a Rose Bouquet.

May I also, on behalf of the Management of the Committee for Tourism in Bulgaria, and all our countrymen, wish good health, happiness and a long life to both your esteemed self and your people.

With the deepest respect.

DIMITAR DOGANOV
Chairman
Bulgarian Committee for Tourism.

helped immeasurably by the wonderful wife at his side. It is a matter of undisputed history that he could scarcely have tackled the burden of kingship at all had it not been for the support and calm confidence of his Queen Consort (today's Queen Elizabeth The Queen Mother) who accepted the unwanted translation from Duchess of York to supreme royal mistress of Buckingham Palace with a courage and determination even outshining the noble glow of her Scottish Bowes-Lyon ancestors. In short, the present Queen was fortunate in an exceptional father and mother.

saw to it that she became educated also in the royal responsibilities and the desk work that were his.

Prince Philip
In the last summer of peace, 1939, Her Royal Highness had paid a visit with her parents to Dartmouth Naval College, and there met, and was shown round the buildings by an 18-year-old Prince Philip of Greece, Lord Mountbatten's good-looking extrovert nephew. Elizabeth was 13. It has always been said that from that time there was, for the Princess, 'no one else'. With

Prince Philip and Princess Elizabeth attend the wedding of Lady Patricia Mountbatten just one year before their own wedding in Westminster Abbey.

Princess Elizabeth's life was fundamentally changed after the 1936 Abdication. From their comfortable family home at 145 Piccadilly the Yorks had to move 'across the Park' and occupy what was at that time a cold and cheerless Palace. And the Princess was Heiress Presumptive. Privately schooled together with her sister Margaret (most of the tutoring was at Windsor Castle in the war years which soon followed), her father

friendship deepening through the years of war, her heart was Philip Mountbatten's.

The Princess began to enter upon the official duties of a public life. At 18 she enlisted in the Auxiliary Territorial Service. As to her private life at home, people in the royal households began to notice that, with increasing frequency, the sports car of Lieutenant Philip, a serving Naval Officer on leave, was at a side entrance to the

Burberrys congratulate Her Majesty on the 40th Anniversary of her reign.

THE BURBERRY —
The World's Best Weatherproof

The ideal Weatherproof for Town or Country,
Sport or Travel.
In a variety of rich pastel shades for ladies.
Hat, shoes and accessories by Burberrys.

BURBERRYS

HAYMARKET · LONDON · S.W.1

Telephone: WHItehall 3343   BURBERRYS LTD

The Tatler and Bystander June 1953

BY APPOINTMENT TO
HER MAJESTY THE QUEEN
WEATHERPROOFERS
BURBERRYS LIMITED
HAYMARKET LONDON

BY APPOINTMENT TO
H.R.H. THE PRINCE OF WALES
OUTFITTERS
BURBERRYS LIMITED
HAYMARKET LONDON

Burberrys
OF LONDON ®

For information please contact: The Wholesale Showroom, Burberrys Limited, 165 Regent Street, London W1R 8AS. Telephone: 071-734 5929.
The Burberry Stores at Haymarket, Regent Street and Knightsbridge, London; Edinburgh, Glasgow, Aberdeen and St Helier, Jersey, Channel Islands.

Palace or at a castle door. When peace came in 1945 it brought a steady shore posting to Philip, and he had more time for meetings with the Princess. The romance blossomed.

Then, in 1947, came the Royal Family's first big post-war journey, an official tour through South Africa. It was during that experience that Elizabeth celebrated her 21st birthday and, in an historic broadcast from a garden in Capetown, spoke to the peoples of the Commonwealth dedicating herself to duty with the words: 'My whole life, whether it be long or short, shall be devoted to your service.'

Her Majesty has more than once publicly recalled that pledge. It is one to which she has been faithful for nearly half a century. *Personal* devotion was in her heart too at that time when she made the speech from South Africa. Her mind, her long-distance letters, her telephone calls were directed to Prince Philip, and in fact she had wished to be officially engaged to him even before the

departure for Capetown. But her father, the King, had insisted — although he approved of the young Mountbatten — that his daughter should go with the family on that overseas tour in order that she should have time fully to consider her long-held desire to become engaged to the man of her choice.

She did not need time: she was only impatient at the separation from Philip, and was 'quite sure' of what both of them wanted. And within two months of the family's arrival back in Britain the betrothal was proclaimed by public announcement. It was popular news. The bridegroom, by then a 25-year-old Royal Navy Lieutenant had been given British citizenship and official

title (though, come to think of it, he was already the picture of a breezy, fair-haired Englishman, and had nothing Greek about him save that his father's name had been Prince Andrew of Greece — and he himself had in fact been born in Corfu, which island he never consciously saw because he was removed from there as a baby. There is no Balkan blood in the Duke of Edinburgh's veins: he had a rather rootless ancestry, a wandering European childhood, and a British schooling. His background was German-Scandinavian, and he (like Elizabeth) was a great-great grandchild of Queen Victoria. The King gave him the title of Duke of Edinburgh on the eve of the wedding to Princess Elizabeth).

The marriage service took place in Westminster Abbey on November 20, 1947. The ceremony and its processions made a gala day in London, the pageantry a heart-warming show of full-dress splendour in a Britain still only gradually emerging from enforced wartime drabness,

Both great-great-grandchildren of Queen Victoria, the newly titled Duke of Edinburgh and Princess Elizabeth married on November 20, 1947.

and still in the grip of rationing: the bride was granted an extra issue of clothing coupons for the buying of materials to make her wedding dress.

For the first year or two of marriage Princess Elizabeth was able to live the life of a naval officer's wife. She went several times to Malta, where the Duke of Edinburgh was stationed; but gradually the failing health of her father caused her to take on an increasing share of the public duties of royalty.

When, in 1948, she gave birth to her first child — Charles, today's Prince of Wales —

The coronation of Queen Elizabeth II was seen by millions of people around the world through the relatively new medium of television.

in Buckingham Palace, the King was lying seriously ill in a nearby room. However, a slow improvement in the monarch's condition was noted, and he seemed to be responding to nursing treatment well enough to tackle duties in public once more, and so he began to undertake some engagements again in London and in nearby parts of the home country. Meantime there were joys in his family life. He took delight in the company of his two small grandchildren (Anne, the second one, the Princess Royal of today, was born in 1950) and was particularly pleased with Princess Elizabeth's agreeable showing as Heiress.

But overseas visits were now out of the question for King George; and in the late autumn of 1951 he sent the Princess and her husband on a visit to Canada in his stead — a six weeks' tour which was exhausting as

well as exhaustive: the outward flight, before the age of the big jet aircraft had dawned, took seventeen hours.

Again, early in the next year, Elizabeth and Philip took the place of the King and Queen for what was to have been a major traverse of Australia and New Zealand. The couple left their children and their home (which then was Clarence House, St. James's Palace, famous for the last four decades as the headquarters of Queen Elizabeth the Queen Mother) and flew out, to Nairobi, from London Airport on a cold last day of that year's January . But they never reached the Antipodes, for it was on the very preliminary stage of the tour — they had only reached Kenya, a bare seven days after the United Kingdom departure — that the Princess received the news of her father's death and her own accession to the Throne.

The Reign Begins

King George VI died, suddenly, in his sleep at Sandringham, on February 6, 1952. Nobody knows the hour of his death. It had been thought that he was making a slow but reassuring recovery; and his passing was a deep shock to his daughter. (Thus it may be added at this point in the royal life-story that, understandably, anniversaries of the date of her accession have been for Her Majesty private days of sombre recollection of loss rather than glad celebration.)

The royal daughter, twenty-five years old, was a thousand miles away from home when she learned of the King's death and that she was at once the new Sovereign. She became Queen, in fact, up a tree in Africa. She and Prince Philip had spent a moonlit Spring night watching wild animals come to a water hole in Kenya's Aberdare Forest game reserve, where their perch was the veranda of a wooden hut 'hotel' high up in the branches of

The young Queen Elizabeth II sets foot on British soil for the first time since the death of her father. Amongst those waiting to greet her was her first prime minister, Winston Churchill.

William Grant & Sons Ltd.

AN INDEPENDENT FAMILY COMPANY FOR FIVE GENERATIONS.

WILLIAM GRANT & SONS CONGRATULATE
HER MAJESTY QUEEN ELIZABETH II
ON THE 40TH ANNIVERSARY
OF HER ACCESSION TO THE THRONE.

a giant fig-tree; and the dire news from London reached her only next morning when back at the hunting lodge where the travellers were staying. The royal party at once left to fly back to a homeland in mourning.

In her luggage were Accession documents, including messages to the British Parliament, which the Princess had carried with her in a sealed envelope during travels ever since the Canadian tour, for there had been a latent fear that they might have been needed then.

So began Britain's Second Elizabethan Reign. At Heathrow, Her Majesty, ashen but composed, came down the aircraft steps on the spot where as Princess she had waved good-bye to her father less than seven days before. Her first Prime Minister, Winston Churchill, was waiting to receive her.

Mr. Churchill, ever loyal to the wearer of the Crown, was soon hailing his Sovereign as 'the young and gleaming champion of a wise and kindly way of life.' But the veteran statesman was never obsequious. Indeed there transpired a conflict of opinion between him and the Queen, during the months of planning for the Coronation, over one important aspect of the historic ceremony. Cabinet and clergy advised the Queen that to televise the Crowning service would threaten the dignity of the occasion and impose an extra strain on Her Majesty — hard to believe though that attitude is today! The P.M. gave the message to the Palace that it was considered not proper for the BBC's live cameras to be in or anywhere near the Abbey's sanctuary or altar. It was only after nine months of doubt and dispute, only after repeated lobbying and careful camera demonstrations, to show how unobtrusive television's men and machines could be, that there came a change of attitude and permission given for pictures to flow 'live' and worldwide from Westminster's famous royal church.

In the end, it was the Queen's personal decision, overruling Archbishop, Earl Marshal, Prime Minister and all. She wished her subjects everywhere to 'be there', to see her and join her throughout the entire sacred and scintillating ritual.

Coronation Day, June the Second 1953, thus brought the 'crowning' of British television. The Abbey ceremonies and also the processions outside were fully covered. It was the day that TV 'came of age'. Millions of people all over the world saw the whole event from those many cameras in London. Any household then possessing such a thing as a television set spent the entire day, neighbours and all, engrossed round those nine-inch screens in crowded rooms. And the broadcasts were an unqualified triumph.

In the autumn that followed, Her Majesty

The Queen grew up with corgis as family pets and the breed has remained a firm favourite.

set out to accomplish, as Queen, the Commonwealth tour she had so briefly begun early in 1952 before her sudden accession. It was, and remains, the longest odyssey of her reign: over fifty thousand miles of travel. She and Prince Philip were away from the United Kingdom for a whole six months. Huge programmes of vivid engagements were carried through in Bermuda, Jamaica, Fiji, Tonga, and in all parts of New Zealand and Australia; then Uganda, Malta and Gibraltar on the way home.

Most of the grand tour was made by sea aboard a liner, the SS *Gothic*, still carrying a fair amount of cargo but part-converted into a pro tem royal yacht, a floating headquarters of the Monarchy, for that special half year. Unusually, the vessel carried officers and men of both the Merchant Service and the Royal Navy, and there was unique communications equipment.

Where, it might be asked, was *Britannia?* The 6,000-ton royal yacht — which the Queen had named and launched at Clydebank in '53 — was in the final stages of completion and trials whilst the Queen was away; and the two young royal children of those days were the first of the Palace family to take passage in the vessel. Prince Charles and Princess Anne, then aged 5 and 3, sailed out from Britain in the shining new ship and met their parents on the harbour of Tobruk when the tour was beginning its concluding stages. So the whole family voyaged triumphantly back in their own maritime palace, through the Mediterranean, the Eastern Atlantic, the English Channel, and up the Thames into the heart of London in May 1954.

That was the first of innumerable tours throughout the Commonwealth and visits, year after year, to a host of foreign countries at the invitation of their governments. Queen Elizabeth long ago became the most travelled and most experienced Head of State in the world. She has learned at first hand. Familiar in any case — day by day, wherever she may be — with people and problems abroad from her study of Cabinet and Foreign Office papers (the famous 'Red boxes'), she also has personal recall of a great variety of countries. In the overall view, it is no exaggeration to say that she has a greater breadth of knowledge of the world about her than any of her ministers possesses.

Nor is there any county of the United Kingdom that she does not know, from visits to its towns and villages, farms and factories, colleges and cultural centres. It has indeed been made apparent that she has kept so well in touch with new develop-

The Queen captured in a comparatively rare moment of relaxation.

ments that every Prime Minister of her reign, after emerging from the weekly 'audience of the Sovereign' many times, has privately confessed to have *gained* during those conversations more in information and good advice from this queen than he took with him into the Palace.

So far, the Queen has had nine Prime Ministers: Churchill, Eden, Macmillan, Douglas-Home, Wilson, Heath, Callaghan, Margaret Thatcher and John Major.

Family Life

Inevitably, the chronicle of these royal years is a record of observable happenings and figures of history, but it should not be imagined that the second Elizabeth's life is all paperwork and politics and pounding round the globe. Personal and outdoor life is very much part of the picture. She is a rich landowner, intensely devoted to horses, their breeding and training and racing. She is assiduous in the supervision of her large homes. And, above all, it has to be said that to her, and to Prince Philip, a main and sustaining job and joy has always been personal domestic and family life: the raising of her children, and now *their* children. From the start, education was given careful attention. Changing with the times in this as in other respects, the royal parents began by making sure that their firstborn, Prince Charles, and his sister in due course, would learn and develop not in a segregated life under governesses and tutors but in the world outside palace walls together with other boys and girls: 'going away to school' — that was a state of affairs which had never happened in the monarchy before.

Princess Anne — who was born at Clarence House, — went away to boarding school in Kent (Benenden) in 1963 when she was thirteen. By that time her brother Charles had had experience as a day boy and a boarder, and was on his way to his 'big school', Gordonstoun, in the distant Grampian region of north-west Scotland.

No longer were Charles and Anne the only children. Nine and a half years after

As Colonel-in-Chief or Captain General the Queen is affiliated to over 40 army regiments worldwide.

Anne's birth, the doctors at the Palace were able to report (in the arcane terms of royal usage) that the Queen had been 'safely delivered of a Prince'. That was February 19, 1960, and the prince was Andrew, today's Duke of York. (Prince Edward, youngest of the family, arrived four years later.) Crowds cheered outside the Palace when the doctors' announcements were posted on the railings.

The biggest excitement and royal news headlines of 1960, however, were occasioned by the wedding of Her Majesty's high-spirited sister, Princess Margaret, to the photographer Anthony Armstrong-Jones (who was created Earl of Snowdon in the following year, thus ennobling the two children of that marriage). The marriage was dissolved in 1979.

For the Queen, the nineteen-sixties were heavy with official work, and domestic weeks had to be tight-packed between months of overseas travel. The mileage of the itineraries which she and her husband the Duke of Edinburgh tackled totalled the circumference of the world several times over. Her Majesty's determination and bravery, her insistence on carrying out ordained visits which acquired potential dangers as they neared, was exemplified several times. In 1961 her advisers were nervous about her going to the troubled republic of Ghana, which was then under

the precarious rule of the first black African prime minister, Kwame Nkrumah. Rioting throngs, defying authority, pulling down statues and shouting against the Crown marred the days immediately before the date of royal arrival. But the Queen flew out to Accra as scheduled — and drove through Accra along clamorous streets to be greeted by deafening cheers of welcome.

Again, in 1967, ministers were fearful about Her Majesty's visit to Quebec City, as part of her salute to Canada's Confederation centennial celebrations, because terrorists and French-Canadian Separatist extremists had announced that they 'would not be responsible for the Queen's safety' if she came. But the threats did not deter a courageous woman from driving, openly and on time, as I remember, from Wolfe's Cove across the historic Heights Of Abraham and into the provincial City in an open car. It was, though, a journey made in an eerie silence because of a strange absence of crowds on the roadsides: the fact was that people had stayed at home in fear of being witnesses to

A large part of the Queen's life is spent touring abroad.

an assassination, and watched the royal progress on television from the safety of their homes. Next day — ashamed, it seemed, at what had happened — French Canada turned out in thousands to wave to the visitors as they drove to Quebec's airport to continue on the next set of engagements for the Queen of Canada.

The year 1965 was only three weeks old when there came the death of Winston Churchill, at the age of 90. At once, the long-planned arrangements for his laying-

A ROYAL SALUTE

Chivas Brothers Ltd is proud
to compliment
Her Majesty Queen Elizabeth II
on the 40th anniversary
of Her ascendency to the throne.

Royal Salute *21 Year Old Scotch Whisky.*

Chivas Regal *12 Year Old Scotch Whisky.*

The Glenlivet *12 Year Old Malt Scotch Whisky.*

Passport *Scotch Whisky.*

100 Pipers *Scotch Whisky.*

to-rest were put in train. Seven years before, the Queen had told her then Prime Minister, Macmillan, that she wished Winston to be accorded a State Funeral — a signal honour for a commoner and the first such occasion since the deaths of Nelson and the great Duke of Wellington.

On January 30, the day of the burial and one of the most bitterly cold days in England anyone could remember, Her Majesty laid aside her routine precedence: she and the Family were waiting with the rest of the congregation inside St. Paul's before the cortege reached the Cathedral. The Queen moreover had provided five of the horse-drawn carriages from the Royal Mews as transport for the ladies of the Churchill family and staff in the wake of the coffin on its gun-carriage which led the slow-paced procession through streets lined by immense crowds and took a full hour to traverse the route from Westminster to Ludgate Hill.

An example of the Queen's thoughtfulness remains in memory from that royal-style funeral day. The passengers — Churchill ladies — in the ancient royal landaus which crawled through the city streets in the bitterly freezing conditions of that January morning might have suffered chillness beyond endurance had not Her Majesty ordered for them not only a score of thick rugs for extra protection but also a hot-water bottle to be put into each person's hands at the moment when the cortege was starting off on its arctic way.

Monarchy and The Media

The reporting, in print and picture, of personal actions and first-hand views of the Queen and the Royal Family is nowadays an accepted feature of the 'projection' of royal affairs. Her Majesty is not just a national icon but a flesh-and-blood person. There exists a fair degree of openness about the public image.

But it was by no means always so. At the beginning of the Queen's reign, although one came across the title of Press Secretary among the members of the official palace Household, a deep suspicion of journalists prevailed. I sometimes had a feeling that if I went too far beyond the crisp formal statements recording official occasions, the words of the Court Circular, I was in danger of a slammed door or a frogmarch to the Tower. But more relaxed relations between royal entourages and the more respectable ranks of writers, broadcasters and photographers soon set in: it was allowed that the Queen was a human being as well as a national symbol, remote upon a pedestal. A busy press office burgeoned with the Private Secretary's department; and today there pervades in it a fresh and healthy public-relations air utterly different from the constrained whiffs bearing curt 'press releases' forty years ago.

The real beginning of the Great Press Changing of the Guard at Buckingham Palace took place in the Sixties on the taking over of the post of Press Officer to the Queen by a young Australian named William Heseltine. He led the way to the present state of reasonably controlled media

The Queen became the first reigning British monarch to visit the Vatican and to meet the Pope.

access to the first family.

In 1968 so many requests were made for filming and interviewing 'the Royals' that, on Heseltine's suggestion and with the Queen's co-operation, unique facilities were granted for the making of a long television 'documentary', simply called *Royal Family*, giving widely located close-up sequences about public activities, but also unexpected, and hugely liked, glimpses of the Queen and her people at home — living a hitherto very private and unpublicised life. A film crew of eight and their cameras and microphones had been 'part of the furniture' travelling the world with Her Majesty. The production was a remarkable break-through in communication and

CHAPTER IV

"I have learnt the way to circum-
navigate the globe; have seen what
may be done and what should be
avoided; what time is required and
the best season for making the
tour; what détours may be made
to the best advantage; what are the
respective denominations and the
proportionate values of moneys of
all the states and countries visited.
In a word, I think I comprehend the
whole of this 'business of pleasure'
around the world."

Thomas Cook

Thomas Cook wrote these words over 100 years ago.
We've been living up to them ever since. All over the world.

The most trusted name in travel.

awareness — and a resounding success. It was in 1969 that *Royal Family* was shown all over the world: a very special salute — and thus a forerunner of the BBC team's new epic documentary, the film '*Elizabeth R*', the screening of which opened the 1992 celebrations of Her Majesty's 40 years' reign.

At this point I ought perhaps to recall that the success of that unprecedented film

It may be, nevertheless, that a good number of people have sensed that Her Majesty, always averse to 'putting on an act', has never become completely at ease when talking to a battery of cameras, even though varied efforts have been made to brighten her Christmas message by interpolating the actual speech with shots from the year's travels and pieces of film showing, for instance, the royal children at home.

The Queen retains links with European royalty. She is pictured here signing the register as godmother to Princess Theodora, daughter of the exiled King Constantine and Queen Anne-Marie of Greece.

of 23 years ago had consequences which had not been foreseen (and maybe the impact and scale of the 1969 production explains the long interval between that documentary and the present one).

Because of the universal screening, and repeating of the '*Royal Family*' opus, and also the full-scale televising of the Investiture of the Prince of Wales at Caernarfon Castle in that same year, the Queen felt that she and her family had perhaps been over 'exposed' and therefore she decided not to broadcast the traditional Sovereign's Christmas message that year. There were widespread protests from listeners and viewers: the annual landmark of December 25 had become 'part of Christmas Day'. So the message was resumed in 1970 and has been delivered ever since.

Incidentally, it is worth noting that Bill Heseltine, the man who as Press Secretary influenced the image of our modern monarchy more than anyone, had a meteoric rise through the high echelons of the servants of the Queen: when he retired from the Palace in 1990 he had become 'Sir William' and was the senior and most experienced Private Secretary to Her Majesty — in effect the most important courtier in the whole Household.

The years of the Seventies and the Queen's third decade saw more desk work and, it has seemed, even more extensive duties overseas. The journeys of Queen and Duke varied from Hawaii to Indonesia, Tonga to Turkey, and — Commonwealth-inclined as this Sovereign resolutely is — months were spent in visits to 'British' territories great and small across the far oceans.

And domestic occurrences, mostly happy but once or twice horrifying, marked those Seventies. The Queen's Silver Jubilee was the big ceremonial event: Her Majesty had been on the Throne for 25 years on February 6, 1977. The great celebrations of the jubilee lasted the whole of that year. Within the twelve month span the royal couple travelled nearly 70,000 miles, seven thousand within the United Kingdom itself.

Four years before that, Princess Anne (now the Princess Royal) was wedded with some splendour to Captain Mark Phillips. This couple have a son and a daughter (Peter Phillips, born in '77, is the Queen's first grandchild), but the marriage ended with an amicable separation in 1989.

An incident of a shocking kind exploded in 1974 when an unstable gunman stopped the car in which Anne and her husband were travelling along London's Mall, and fired a number of bullets whilst shouting that he wanted to kidnap the Princess. Her police officer and another man were

Numerous portraits have been painted of the Queen. This portrait by Noakes is part of the Royal Collection.

wounded, but Anne was miraculously untouched, though fired-at repeatedly.

Personal shock of a different nature came into the news in 1979 when it was found that the long-established Surveyor of the Queen's Pictures, the art expert, the late Sir Anthony Blunt, was a traitor and was suddenly unmasked after years of spying for Soviet Russia. Her Majesty's disgust that such a double-dealer had been employed in her household may be imagined: the outward sign was that he was summarily sacked and stripped of his knighthood.

Then came the Eighties, with the Queen's 60th birthday celebrations in the middle of the decade which her mother's 80th had begun. Political upheavals notwithstanding, this was a joyous period in the history books. Gala events were the wedding of the Prince of Wales to Lady Diana Spencer in 1981 and of Prince Andrew to Sarah Ferguson five years later. For Andrew's marriage the royal dukedom of York was revived and bestowed on him. In the interval between those marriages the two Wales' princes were born: William in 1982 and Harry two years later — sons of Charles and next after him in the direct line of Succession.

An unexpected turn in the Palace family's life was the sudden, and not domestically popular, decision of the Queen's youngest son Prince Edward, new out of university, to break tradition and resign from the uniformed Services — the Royal Marines in his case — and pursue a civilian career, getting a job in the world of commercial theatre. This did not last as a full-time occupation, though his patronage of Youth Theatre enterprises continues. New turns in this young man's career are probably still to come, but, in any event, Edward has for some time now been working hard for special projects of his father's famous worldwide Duke of Edinburgh's Award Scheme for young people. Perhaps it is permissible to imagine that this dutiful labour by the son is benignly regarded by the father as atonement: the Duke is Captain General of the Corps of Royal Marines.

Personal diaries of Buckingham Palace people during the nineteen-eighties no doubt recorded some international history in itemising Argentina's invasion of the Falklands, for it was in the fighting in the subsequent campaign to liberate the islands that HRH Prince Andrew won his spurs as a naval helicopter pilot.

Whether an almost unbelievable incident deep inside the Palace in the mid-July of the same year, 1982, has made the diaries is a private matter. But the happening was without parallel, and it certainly caused a shake-up in the systems and personnel of policing and security at the big house. At seven o'clock one morning the Queen was awakened to find a

garden, and no other servant or policeman was at that moment on hand. Her Majesty pressed the night-alarm bell and tried to telephone the police office, but with no result for some time. She managed to keep the invader talking and then to accompany him into the corridor until help came. The first aid to arrive was not a posse of uniformed bobbies, but a housemaid who happened to enter the corridor, and who, on beholding her employer and the highly agitated man beside her, exclaimed 'Bloody 'ell, Ma'am, what's 'e doin' in 'ere!'

What indeed! A Royalty Protection group organised by the Metropolitan Police has been on Palace duty ever since that

A 41-gun salute in Hyde Park marks the Queen's birthday each year on April 21.

dishevelled, half-crazed man, babbling incoherently, inside her bedroom and trying to draw back the window curtains. The stranger — who proved to be a simple-minded unemployed labourer — had been able to climb walls and drainpipes and to enter the vast headquarters of the monarchy without much difficulty, thanks to extraordinary flaws in constabulary duty and electronic security devices, and had been wandering through a variety of rooms during the night quite unchallenged. He proceeded to sit on the Queen's bed and pour out his troubles to a marvellously calm Monarch. She was alone. The duty footman was walking the corgis in the

episode. And — such are the terrorist dangers nowadays — extra precautions, not generally discernible, are put into operation when royal public engagements are being carried out. It is so with all public figures.

Troubled Times
The most recent years of Her Majesty's term of office have brought violent upheavals in the world scene: the breaching of the infamous Berlin Wall in 1989 and the uniting of a new Germany; the shadows of other Continental struggles; the traumas of Britain's approaches to close involvement in The New Europe's disarray; the crisis and

international Gulf War in the Middle East during the autumn of 1990 and the early months of '91; and then, dwarfing everything else, the cataclysmic break-up of the vast Communist empire of what had for decades been the Soviet Union of Russia — these events and earthquakes have of course been of unprecedented concern to Queen Elizabeth II, as head of our unique Sovereign state. And deep anxiety over the turmoils of Russian disintegration inevitably continues. Democracy instead of autocracy is not an easy change.

Even so, it would be unbalanced not to remember that happier occurrences have lightened the picture in months not long past: the 91st birthday of the still energetic Queen Mother for one thing.

Internationally, the autumn of 1991 brought a brightening of African skies by the welcomed State visit of the Queen and Prince Philip to Zimbabwe, the former Southern Rhodesia, an immensely changed part of the Commonwealth in which Her Majesty had not set foot since she was there as a young princess with her father and mother on that memorable post-war tour of 1947. This time, it was regarded as a mark of stability after years of trouble that the Queen could now be

A grandmother six times over the Queen visits her eldest grandson, Peter Phillips, at his school.

there at all, and that she could stay in the capital city of Harare (which she had known as Salisbury long ago) and attend the 1991 'Summit' there — the Commonwealth Heads of Government Meeting.

The future will undoubtedly bring still more upheavals, or changes in power balances, to the African continent as well as to Europe. But whatever happens in this new decade, it seems sure that the British Throne — in the personal as well as the political sense — will be in the limelight, and may be a focus of hope too.

This is not to suggest change of *occupant* of the hereditary office. Prince Charles, the Heir, is in no way saying 'Move over, Mum'. He has described his mother The Queen as 'terribly sensible and wise'; and those who know him are sure his wish is to see her continue to be the conscientious and effective protagonist of the centuries-old play called British Monarchy — and not merely *acting* the part for she is unaffectedly and beneficially 'being herself' as sincerely today as she was 40 years ago. So — No Abdication (the 1936 event was one weak man's aberration). To quote Lord Home, a former Prime Minister: 'It would be a dangerous and undesirable precedent. Once is enough.'

In any case, Her Majesty's broadcast of Christmas 1991 dispelled any misguided gossip-column speculations that she might be intending to step down from her post. Other people may have forgotten — but she has not — that 40 years ago she inherited and accepted a 'job for life'. At her coronation she was annointed to serve the country as long as she lives — and she has always taken her vows to heart. So, at Christmas she ended her message with the words: 'With your prayers, and your help, and with the love and support of my family, I shall try to serve you in the years to come'.

To those people who question the hereditary nature of the Monarchy's continuity it may be said — dispassionately and at the same time thankfully today — that, although such a process of succession is bound to be a genetic lottery, the lottery this time has, in the present Queen, given the nation a first prize. Even the critics who regard reigning Royalty as an anachronism and a bore may be glad, in years to come, of our monarchy's sensible and intelligent Head as an asset on which to hold fast in the Britain-in-Europe of the Nineties.

So long as Her Majesty's advisers at the Palace and in her Ministries do their part in keeping the Throne's balance between dignity and approachability, protecting private life and yet promoting public lustre, the calming continuance of Queen Elizabeth II's reign in the way manifest during these last four momentous decades will be stamina for her country's future, both national and international.

An official portrait by Karsh of Ottawa of HM The Queen and HRH Prince Philip photographed in the White Drawing Room at Buckingham Palace.

Four decades ago, we carried
the news to the four corners.

CABLE & WIRELESS

THE NEW ELIZABETHAN AGE

Roland Gribben recalls the way we were that historic day in 1952 when Queen Elizabeth II came to the throne, and how dramatically the face of Britain has changed in the four decades since.

At the dawning of the second Elizabethan Age forty years ago beer was 1s 3d a pint (the equivalent of 6.25p today). The average wage for a manual worker was 184s 9d a week (£9.23). And the first automatic electric coffee pot was developed by Bill Russell and Peter Hobbs in Croydon.

The inflatable life jacket was developed after 10 years' research by the RAF. John Cobb was killed on Loch Ness racing a new custom-built turbojet boat at 240mph.

Achievement, whether in the laboratory or in the field of artistic or sporting endeavour, has been the consistent thread running through the first four decades of the new Elizabethan Age — four decades of enormous social and economic change and turmoil, but forty years of tremendous progress in the worlds of technology and science.

The accession of Queen Elizabeth II in 1952 generated an air of expectancy and a patriotic revival that politicians could not hope to match with promises.

A map of the world still showed a distinctive red colouring, and Britain's industrial as well as diplomatic role was still considerable despite the ravages of war and the hangover of the ration book. Austin of Birmingham was helping a company called Nissan of Japan get on its feet again.

The 40th anniversary comes as the new European order of the single market and a new currency beckons, and with an election around the corner. Traditional pageantry will be at a premium. Instead a more reflective, relaxed approach will characterise the celebrations. Pomp and circumstance will be confined to a special exhibition of royal memorabilia at the Victoria and Albert Museum.

The Royal Anniversary Trust, the co-ordinating body set up to mark the event, is anxious to emphasis the lasting benefits produced by four decades of achievement and innovation, using the monarchy as the thread.

The celebrations will conclude in mid-October with a television spectacular marking achievements over the past forty years.

The decades from 1952-1992 embrace some of the most outstanding achievements of the 20th century.

Turn the clock back to the night of February 6 1952 when Princess Elizabeth heard that her father had died and she was Queen of England. There were not satellites to speed the message to a remote hillside in Kenya where she had taken a break during a visit with Prince Philip.

She flew back to London in a BOAC Argonaut from Entebbe via Libya and was greeted at London airport by Mr Churchill,

Rationing was still in force for certain products at the beginning of this reign.

Mr Eden, Foreign Secretary, Mr Attlee, leader of the Opposition, and Mr Clement Davies, Liberal leader.

The Queen drove to Buckingham Palace via Bath Road and the A4 Great West Road.

It was an era when Ivor Novello's 20 horsepower Rolls-Royce was sold for £1,200. A new Silver Dawn cost £4,605. A gallon of petrol was the equivalent of 16p. Hilda Margaret Roberts had been married to Denis Thatcher for four months.

Kenya is now a republic within the Commonwealth. BOAC has given way to British Airways and the Argonaut to Boeing 747s which fly the 4,127 miles to London non-stop in 8½ hours. The journey in 1952 took 19½ hours.

Heathrow is now the busiest international airport in the world, and is run by BAA, and the M4 is the main route into London.

Ration books have disappeared along with hire purchase controls, but VAT is adding 17.5p in the pound to many household items, and a 1952 pound would buy only a thimbleful of British Rail tea. It is worth 6.4p.

The Comet jet airliner, now masquerading as the RAF Nimrod, joins the Queen in a 40th anniversary celebration this year.

The 1992 equivalent of the 1952 Silver Dawn, the Rolls-Royce Silver Spirit, costs

The way we were — the Queen meets victims of the Kent floods in 1953.

1956 14" B&W T.V.

We just missed your Coronation but we weren't going to miss your 40th Anniversary.

1992 107cm COLOUR T.V. CMT 4200

£99,990.15p and the average weekly wage of a manufacturing worker is around £300.

Other things have not changed. The national characteristic of self-denigration is still firmly embedded, and the ability to pioneer and invent — despite the frustrations produced by a lack of resources, under-investment, the brian drain and the decline in manufacturing — is with us. But foreign companies all too often have reaped the rewards of British inventions. Forty years

the birth of new industries with a dynamism and international dimension of their own — electronics, telecommunications, aerospace and North Sea oil and gas.

The computer revolution has invaded the home as well as the factory and office.

The rapid development of banking, insurance and the whole financial service sector has transformed the City of London.

Rationalisation, recession, mergers and liquidations may have seen the disap-

The development of the aircraft industry has revolutionised travel in the last 40 years.

ago manufacturing industry accounted for 40 per cent of national wealth as reflected in the measurement of gross domestic product.

Today it is under 25 per cent, and Britain only accounts for eight per cent of world trade in manufactured goods against 25 per cent in 1952. But GDP over the period has risen from £14.6 billion to £550.5 billion.

The whole industrial and trade base has shifted radically, producing changes in the regional map in the process.

The industries that helped forge the industrial revolution — steel, coal, shipbuilding and textiles — are considerably leaner and in most cases fitter.

European Community rather than Commonwealth markets now take over 50 per cent of British exports. But the disappearance of the old has been accompanied by

pearance of many well-known companies over the past 40 years, but Britain — in native or Anglo-Dutch form — is still home to 15 out of the top 20 European companies.

What is the most outstanding achievement over the period? Concorde? The peaceful development of atomic power? Or an idea that germinated over a kitchen sink and revolutionised the glass industry?

The Harrier jump jet? Or maybe Sir Christopher Cockerell and the hovercraft from an experiment with tin cans?

Prof John Durant, assistant director at the Science Museum, plumps for the achievements of Crick and Watson in establishing the structure of DNA at Cambridge's Cavendish laboratory almost 40 years ago. "It was the most important biological achievement of the century," he says.

PRINCE PHILIP

Tim Heald, author of The Duke (Hodder & Stoughton) profiles the man who has been at the Queen's side throughout her reign and who has had considerable influence on the monarchy as we know it today.

A lifetime in the limelight takes its toll and can make a one dimensional parody of the most complex of individuals. Prince Philip is no exception. There are times when the Duke of Edinburgh of the tabloid press, of Private Eye and Spitting Image seems to have taken over the real person so that even quite intelligent people come to believe the fiction. We have been shown the caricature so often that we have lost sight of the reality.

He has, for example, together with the Right Reverend Michael Mann, published several books of theological debate. Much of the Duke's discourse in them is as acerbic as his public reputation would suggest but the content also includes lengthy quotations from Darwin, dissections of a lecture by Sir Fred Hoyle and of contemporary works such as "Man's Origin, Man's Destiny" and a lively interest in God, Creation, Good and Evil and all manner of subjects light years away from the polo field or the controls of the Royal aircraft. His propensity for boarding the preacher after church services and arguing over details of the sermon is something of a family joke. He loves argument but what many people fail to realise is that this is fuelled as much by real curiosity about knowledge and ideas as it is by his naturally combative temperament.

HRH The Prince Philip Duke of Edinburgh, KG, KT, OM, GBE.

He has read Marx and Jung. He even enjoys poetry though when asked about it, refuses to discuss his taste on the grounds that his views would be too old fashioned and conventional. I know that, like his son, he admires Shakespeare, from whom he quite often quotes in his speeches. I know he likes Dylan Thomas. He seems ambivalent about T.S. Eliot.

Yet this softer side of his nature is one that is seldom displayed, and when revealed comes as a surprise even to members of his own family. It often seems to be assumed that the thoughtful artistic genes with which Prince Charles is credited come only from his mother's side of the family but this is simply not so. A friend of the Duke's once showed me a private letter talking about modern architects and architecture in almost precisely the same vein as Prince Charles — written years before the Prince of Wales charged into that particular arena. And you might think, from the way it is discussed, that Prince Charles was the first member of the Royal Family ever to pick up a paint brush. In fact you could argue that the Duke is a more accomplished artist than the Prince. Unlike his son, Philip favours oils and though his style is robust his subjects can be both domestic and romantic. His subjects have even included the Queen at breakfast

 **Schroders**

For forty years
Her Majesty the Queen's and
H.R.H. the Duke of Edinburgh's
integrity, continuity and
encouragement of stability
in a changing world
have been an example
to everyone in
Schroders' worldwide operations.

and a bunch of gladioli. They are both charming and revealing.

It is not surprising that the Duke is surprising if you believe in the influence of heredity and childhood. He was exiled from Corfu, the island of his birth when he was only eighteen months old, an event which his elder sister Sophie still recalls with spine tingling vividness though he himself disparages its importance on the grounds that he was too young to know what was going on. His early childhood was spent in relatively reduced circumstances in St. Cloud. With four much older sisters he was the baby of the family. Between December 1930 and August 1931 all the sisters married and the family disintegrated with his mother suffering a nervous breakdown and his father, already a somewhat *decontracté* figure opting out and moving to Monte Carlo. Philip commuted between various schlosses and castles and mansions in Britain and Europe and even shunted between the conventional English middle class preparatory school of Cheam and Salem, the pioneering school on the shores of Lake Constance begun by his sister's father-in-law, the Margrave of Baden and Kurt Hahn later his headmaster at Gordonstoun.

In England his original protector and surrogate father was his uncle George, Marquess of Milford Haven, and not as is commonly thought, his other uncle, Lord Mountbatten. But in 1938 Milford Haven died of cancer in his mid-forties. Another particularly close relationship was with his sister Cecile and her husband George Donatus of Hesse. They were both killed, with their young sons, in an air crash at Ostend when Philip was in his teens. The pictures of him at their funeral, a slim fair haired boy in a suit surrounded by a sea of thick German military greatcoats are extraordinarily poignant.

Circumstances therefore combined to make him remarkably self contained and set apart as a young man. He fitted no imaginable mould. More royal, on exact genealogical grounds, than the Princess he was to marry, he was, to the British public at least, an unknown young naval officer without even a surname, when he first began to be noticed as a potential Elizabethan suitor in 1947. The traditional courtiers, referred to disparagingly by one member of the Royal Family as "the men with moustaches", were suspicious and

sometimes downright hostile. To them it did not matter that he had fought a distinguished war with a mention in dispatches. They pointed to his numerous German relations; they resented his un-Englishness; and a quality they could not quite define but which was sometimes described as arrogance. He wasn't easy and he did not conform.

The marriage itself has always, inevitably, been a subject of gossip. Even during the war society figures like Chips Channon and Freda Dudley Ward were propagating rumours of the match. These tales still infuriate the Duke and Chips Channon is still not a name to conjure with in his

Prince Philip is an accomplished artist, preferring oils to watercolours.

company. Then, once he was married, new rumours started. The very people who once gossiped about the possibility of a romance now began to whisper about a "rift".

It is, of course, true that the Queen and the Duke spend much time apart. This is part of the job. The Duke was, for more than twenty years President of the International Equestrian Federation (FEI) and still presides over the World Wide Fund for Nature as he has done since 1964. Since the Duke of Edinburgh's Award Scheme first started in 1956 he has given that as much time as possible. These three interests are his own and not, as a rule, shared with the Queen. When he presents Awards at St. James' Palace he does so on his own; when he visits WWF sponsored projects in far corners of the world he does not take the Queen with him; and she does not join in his carriage driving.

On the other hand they also spend a great deal of time together. The Duke is invariably at his wife's shoulder on the great occasions of state, sometimes — as at the

State Opening of Parliament, actually holding her hand physically as well as metaphorically. Weekends at Windsor; summers at Balmoral; these are shared husband and wife occasions, and although as courtiers always point out there are closed doors behind which no-one can penetrate all the indications are that the Queen and the Duke continue to have a close and mutually supportive relationship. It may not be one which strikes recognisable chords in

constitutional position from which to abdicate so that he does not have to endure the sort of speculation surrounding his wife's job. He can just gradually wind down without anyone much noticing.

Not that he is the sort of man one can imagine calling for slippers and pipe. He is far too restless. He says that he never made a coherent plan when he first took on the role of consort — he still has not had the title "Prince Consort" officially conferred — and

Since giving up the game of polo in 1971, Prince Philip has taken up four-in-hand carriage driving, representing Britain at European and world events.

the hearts of those who commute daily on a nine-to-five basis and whose wives always have something ready in the oven for their return. It is, by definition, a highly visible and unusual marriage, but there is nothing to suggest that it doesn't work rather well.

Now that he is over seventy there are actually indications that he is slowing down. He has already given up helicopter flying and talks of no longer piloting fixed wing aircraft, though his friend and colleague, ten years his senior, Prince Bernhard of the Netherlands still pilots his plane. He has stepped down from the FEI: he has co-opted Prince Edward to the Award Scheme; he has let it be known that the next Commonwealth Study Conference which he first started in the early fifties will be the last one chaired by him. Luckily, for him, there is no

by the same token is not particularly interested in looking back nor in what other people may think of him. (Despite his protestations I think he cares quite a lot about what the rest of us think — otherwise he wouldn't read the morning papers so avidly!)

One of his greatest achievements is that almost half a century after first becoming involved with the British crown the Duke is still having fun — or giving a very convincing imitation of a man having fun. He seems always to have lived at full tilt with bags of zest and enthusiasm, an attitude which, though questioning, has always been positive and — not necessarily to be expected in one who was emphatically not born British — patriotic. Despite the anomalies in his position vis-a-vis the Queen we should never forget that he is her husband

and the father of the modern Royal Family and without him it would be a very different institution. His influence has not always been one who has coloured the national life for many years. Because he is so often pictured on formal occasions walking respectfully and

With his Queen of 40 years and his wife of almost 45 years, Prince Philip enjoys a 70th birthday salute.

visible but it has always been there.

Many years ago he once complained plaintively that he was being pressured into becoming little more than a "bloody amoeba" but he has never ever been that. He has managed despite the odds to be recognisably, distinctively a person in his own right and deferentially behind the Queen people sometimes assume that this is all he does and that his job stops here. Nothing could be further from the truth. It is a measure of his achievement that if there wasn't a Prince Philip, Duke of Edinburgh, many people would feel a compelling need to invent one.

STANDARD LIFE

CONGRATULATES

HER

MAJESTY

Queen Elizabeth II

ON THE 40TH

ANNIVERSARY

OF HER

ACCESSION TO

THE THRONE.

Standard Life

THE FAMILY FIRM

It was Prince Philip who coined the phrase 'The Firm' when talking of the Royal Family. Indeed as Brian Hoey, author of 'Monarchy: Behind The Scenes with the Royal Family' shows, it is a true reflection of a hard working team, who seem tireless in their enthusiasm and energy for their work.

Prince Charles once said that everything worth having has to be 'worked at' from marriage to the Commonwealth, and Her Majesty The Queen, in the forty years she has been on the Throne, has made sure that her family has always worked to support the ideal of the Monarchy.

received at Buckingham Palace addressed to various members of 'The Firm' hoping that she or he will attend an assortment of functions, make speeches or simply grace an event with their presence.

Obviously it would be impossible to accept every one, but even so, the number

Since he left the Royal Navy in 1976 the Prince of Wales' life has been filled with public duties.

There is nothing unusual in the idea of a working family in the latter part of the twentieth century; indeed, it would be far more unusual to find a family that did not need to work. But the workload of the Royal Family is such that it would be impossible for the Queen alone to carry out the thousands of public engagements, at home and overseas, that the senior members of the Royal Family attend every year.

Public interest in Britain's Royal Family has grown to such an extent that in any one year around fifty thousand invitations are

grows each year with the Queen carrying out the major portion — some 500 commitments at home and abroad. During the 40 years she has been on the Throne, Queen Elizabeth II has become the most widely travelled and easily recognised monarch the world has ever seen. By the time of her Silver Jubilee in 1977 she had seen and been seen by more of her subjects than all her predecessors put together.

During the early years of her reign the Queen was helped in carrying out her many public duties mainly by her husband, the

Duke of Edinburgh, by her sister, Princess Margaret, and by Queen Elizabeth the Queen Mother. However these days the workload has been spread a little wider as the younger members of the Royal Family have reached the age when they can undertake duties on their own.

Nevertheless it is the immediate Royal Family that most people want to see. So the bulk of Royal engagements are carried out by the Queen herself, the Duke of

festivals' around which the rest of the year revolves. For example, every year since her Coronation in 1953 Queen Elizabeth has travelled overseas on official visits, and while she is away with part of her Household, other members of her staff remain in Britain preparing for the domestic programme.

More than 80 functions a year are held at Buckingham Palace alone. These range from informal lunches given on a monthly basis by the Queen for about a dozen people, to

The Princess of Wales is Patron or President of more than thirty organisations and takes a keen interest in children.

Edinburgh, the Prince and Princess of Wales, the Queen Mother and by the Queen's only daughter The Princess Royal, who is second only to her mother in the number of Royal engagements she undertakes. The Queen's second son, the Duke of York, together with his wife, the Duchess, carries out a small number of public duties when his service commitments in the Royal Navy permit. Prince Edward, the youngest of the Queen's four children has also started to take his place in 'the Royal Firm' while Princess Margaret, Princess Alexandra, the Kents and Gloucesters also have full programmes of public engagements.

Arranging the Royal Family's working year takes place in June and December, when the many requests are discussed and decisions about them taken. There are certain 'fixed

the three annual Garden Parties in the summer, each attended by up to 9,000 guests who have been drawn from all walks of life.

The normal yearly programme of the Sovereign includes 14 Investitures at which she awards honours to a total of just over 2,000 men and women, and then of course, there are the State Occasions when the Queen is the central figure. The State Opening of Parliament, for example, is a glittering ceremonial attended by peers in their robes and bishops in their ecclesiastical gowns as well as the full ceremonial compliment. It is also the only occasion when the Queen wears a crown, the Imperial State Crown, brought from the Tower of London for the day.

And earlier each year, the Trooping the Colour ceremony takes place in London

Princess Anne works tirelessly for the Save The Children Fund.

FINE ART DEVELOPMENTS P.L.C.

Extends to
Her Majesty...

Congratulations

...on providing
40 years
of leadership
to our Nation

WORKING FOR THE COMMUNITY

AS THE U.K.'S LARGEST SUPPLIER
OF CHARITY TRADING SERVICES,
LAST YEAR
WE HELPED CHARITIES RAISE £11m
THROUGH THE SALE OF
CARDS AND GIFTS
PLUS DONATIONS OF £1.7m

● **FINE ART DEVELOPMENTS P.L.C.** ●
GREETING CARDS · STATIONERY · MAIL ORDER · CHARITY SERVICES
DAWSON LANE, BRADFORD BD4 6HW

The Duchess of York, one of the newer members of the Royal Family.

He also holds senior appointments in the armed services and devotes much of his time to the conservation of the countryside and the state of the environment, both in Britain and throughout the world.

Over a quarter of a century ago he conceived the idea of the Duke of Edinburgh Award Scheme which is intended to help both the young, and those people who take an interest in their welfare. It is designed as an introduction to leisure time activities, a challenge to the individual to personal achievement, and as a guide to those people and organisations who are concerned about the development of our future citizens. Fascinated by advanced technology, Prince Philip also serves on a number of committees with scientific interests. He has also accompanied the Queen on every overseas tour since 1952.

Since he left the Royal Navy in 1976 the Prince of Wales' life has been crowded with

during the Queen's Official Birthday Parade. Her Majesty has two birthdays; her own and the Official Birthday of the Sovereign, usually the second Saturday in June. This is as a result of King Edward VII, born in November when the British weather was considered unsuitable for a birthday parade. It was decided to hold a formal celebration in the summer when members of the public could enjoy the spectacle.

Throughout the year diplomatic representatives of various countries are received by the Queen on arrival in Britain, usually accompanied by their wives and members of their staff, who are also presented to Her Majesty.

Every week while Parliament is sitting, the Prime Minister is received in audience to discuss affairs of State and the Queen is also given a daily account of proceedings in Parliament. The amount of paperwork she gets through is prodigious. Wherever the Queen is in the world the paperwork follows her. The work of Monarchy never stops. Rarely does she get through a single day without working at her desk for two or three hours.

Assisting the Queen are other members of the Royal Family who also have full calendars of events.

The Duke of Edinburgh, for instance, acts as patron or president to many organisations.

The Duke of York is a long term career officer in the Navy but undertakes public duties whenever possible.

public duties and his diary rarely has a vacant date.

A great deal of his time is spent working for charitable organisations, two of which are particular favourites, The Prince's Trust, which helps with the provision of facilities for

The Olayan Group

Suliman S Olayan KBE
Chairman

PO Box 8772
Riyadh 11492
Saudi Arabia

Her Majesty Queen Elizabeth II

Your Majesty

On behalf of myself and my associates at The Olayan Group, may I offer warmest congratulations and best wishes on the fortieth anniversary of your Accession.

Although the world has seen many changes since 1952, the principles you have upheld throughout your reign with such consummate dignity and grace have been an inspiration and example to us all. The message in your annual broadcasts touches the hearts of people around the world.

The Olayan Group shares in and benefits from the historic and abiding ties which exist between Great Britain and Saudi Arabia. As we pursue our commercial, industrial and financial business worldwide, we shall work to strengthen those ties and demonstrate our affection and esteem for the nation your Majesty leads.

I have the honour to remain

Respectfully

Olayan

OLAYAN

young people; and the Prince of Wales' Committee, which encourages practical projects involving voluntary participation. These are not bodies to which he merely lends

Colleges, the Presidency of which the Prince took over in 1978, from the late Earl Mountbatten of Burma. It is an international movement which aims to promote

Prince Edward plays a more and more active role in the Duke of Edinburgh's Award Scheme which his father set up in 1956.

Despite being in her 92nd year, the Queen Mother is still an active, and much loved member of 'the firm'.

his name as a figurehead, chairman in every sense of the word, he involves himself actively. Another favourite is the United World

peace and understanding through education which the Prince takes a keen interest in and is always delighted when former pupils

Princess Margaret took over the presidency of the Girl Guides Association from the Queen in 1965.

approach him on one of his overseas tours.

Like other members of the Royal Family, he has close links with the armed forces and he is associated with several regiments in the army. He also holds senior ranks in both the Royal Air Force and the Royal Navy.

The Princess of Wales is the mother of two young children, Prince William and Prince Henry — yet she also manages to carry out many public duties. Her principal interests lie with the handicapped, the deaf and the elderly. She is patron or president of more than thirty organisations, and she rarely refuses an invitation to help. She has taken the time to learn sign language giving her an insight into the problems experienced by the hard of hearing.

The Queen's only daughter, the Princess Royal, combines a wide variety of roles in her public life. Two favourite causes are the Save the Children Fund and the Riding for the Disabled Association, for whom she will go anywhere and talk to anyone — as long as the charities benefit. She is a Counsellor of State and Chancellor of London University, an elected position in which she succeeded Queen Elizabeth the Queen Mother.

She has undertaken a number of particularly arduous tours in Africa and South East Asia, visiting Save the Children Fund projects to see famine relief work at first hand. As a former Olympic horse-woman, she took part in the 1976 Olympic Games in Montreal; she is currently President of the British Olympic Association and a member of the International Olympic Committee, as well as President of FEI (Federation Equestrienne Internationale).

The Queen's second son, the Duke of York, is a long term career officer in the Royal Navy, serving as a helicopter pilot instructor. His wife, the former Miss Sarah Ferguson, combines her public life with being the mother of two small daughters. Both the Duke and Duchess undertake public duties in Britain and abroad, subject to His Royal Highness's service commitments.

Prince Edward, the Queen's youngest son is active in the Duke of Edinburgh's Award Scheme and is a successful fund-raiser for charity. In 1990 he succeeded his father as President of the Commonwealth Games Federation. Together with his brothers and sister, he is a Counsellor of State, standing in for the Queen at meetings of the Privy Council when she is abroad, and receiving

The Duchess of Kent is known for her warm and caring nature.

diplomats and other distinguished visitors.

Queen Elizabeth The Queen Mother has not slackened her work pace, even though she is now in her tenth decade. She is associated with hundreds of organisations and active in many still managing to attend a large number of official functions every year.

The Queen's sister Princess Margaret, Countess of Snowdon, is artistic by nature, and gravitates towards the arts where she is patron of numerous theatrical endeavours.

The Duke and Duchess of Gloucester carry out a substantial number of public engagements.

Then there is the Duke of Kent, an accomplished linguist, who lends his unique talents to a variety of enterprises connected with Britain's export drive, while the Duchess is known for her personal visits to hospices and a warm and caring nature.

The Duke and Duchess of Gloucester, together with Princess Alice, the second oldest member of the Royal Family, have causes of their own which they support, in addition to helping the Queen with her public duties.

Prince and Princess Michael of Kent — he is a keen linguist.

Busy 'royals' too are Prince and Princess Michael of Kent, (the Prince is another linguist) and Princess Alexandra, one of the most likeable and sought after members of the family.

This then is Britain's working Royal Family today: conscientious, hard working and industrious who tend to divide their activities through a preference for particular subjects rather than a formal predetermined allocation. The only exception to this rule is the Queen herself who is allowed no

Princess Alexandra — one of the most popular members of the Royal family.

personal preference. But she has led by personal example in her private and public lives and she has carved for herself a unique position throughout the world. Although there are other female sovereigns in several countries whenever one hears a reference to "the Queen" there is never a moment's doubt in anyone's mind that this could mean only one person — Elizabeth II.

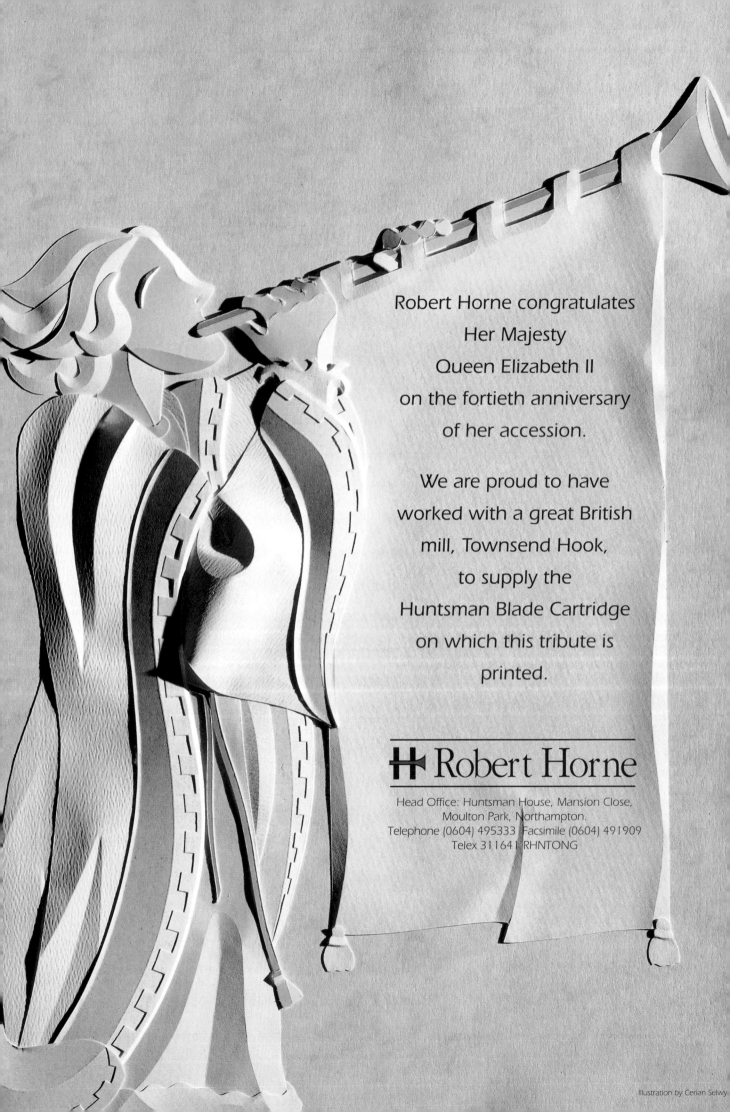

Robert Horne congratulates
Her Majesty
Queen Elizabeth II
on the fortieth anniversary
of her accession.

We are proud to have
worked with a great British
mill, Townsend Hook,
to supply the
Huntsman Blade Cartridge
on which this tribute is
printed.

Robert Horne

Head Office: Huntsman House, Mansion Close,
Moulton Park, Northampton.
Telephone (0604) 495333 Facsimile (0604) 491909
Telex 311641 RHNTONG

Illustration by Cerian Selwy

THE WORKING YEAR

The Queen's working day is a busy mixture of affairs of state, fixed appointments and one-off events as well as making time when possible for personal interests and relaxation. Ronald Allison, CVO, former Press Secretary to the Queen looks at how the Royal year is planned.

A typical day in the life of the Queen? I am not sure there is such a thing. After all 'typical' is not a word often used when talking of the monarch — except in the sense that a look or gesture or an act of kindness might be described as being 'typical of her'. Certainly she is not a 'typical' woman and while she does combine a career with being a wife and a mother she does so in a way all her own. And when you think about it the Queen is not even a typical sovereign — who else is Head of State of more than a dozen independent nations as well as being a fully involved Head of the Commonwealth?

So instead of looking for an unchanging daily routine, consider the variety of working days the Queen fits into any one year. Mind you, a year as a whole will have a pattern that might be said to be 'typical' of the past forty, for the Queen is happy with familiar and regular events and most enjoys being in surroundings she knows and loves well. Thus the Queen's diary will always have a number of fixed dates which will be among the first to be put in place by her Private Secretary. The New Year at Sandringham, Maundy Thursday, Easter at Windsor, Trooping the Colour on the Queen's official birthday followed by 'Garter' day at Windsor and then Royal Ascot. The garden parties in July, the Western Isles cruise each August, work on the way, but, then, Balmoral. November, with the State Opening of Parliament and Remembrance

Red boxes are an integral part of the daily routine of the Queen wherever she might be.

weekend and, then, on to Christmas, most often in the present reign spent at Windsor.

It is into that framework that go the days that make the Queen's life so varied — days that may be spent in Buckingham Palace with no outside engagements, days overseas on a state visit or Commonwealth tour, days in the United Kingdom on tours involving the Queen's Flight or the Royal Train, or days during the breaks from official engagements but which nevertheless are never free of official business.

Ah yes, the official business — the affairs of state that do indeed dominate the Queen's working life. Every day, wherever she may be, the Queen receives reports from her Ministers at home and her representatives overseas, in both Commonwealth and foreign countries. These come in various forms — telegrams, letters, despatches — and together with them come Submissions which have to be read and signed. Some two hundred letters a day would be about the norm for the Queen and no day ends without there being some papers to be read and signed. It might be possible for all this to be done hurriedly and superficially but that is not the Queen's way. Twice every day, morning and evening, the paper work is delivered to the Queen in those famous red boxes — envelopes really but what solid, impressive envelopes those boxes are!

In June of 1991 a day the Queen spent in Buckingham Palace involved her in all the usual official business, gave her time

NATIONAL COMMERCIAL BANK
JAMAICA LIMITED

A MEMBER OF THE NCB GROUP OF COMPANIES

In Tribute To Her Majesty

On behalf of the Directors,
Management and Staff of
National Commercial Bank Jamaica Limited,
I have the honour to convey
to Her Majesty, Queen Elizabeth,
our warmest congratulations
on the 40th Anniversary
of Her accession to the Throne.

We wish Her Majesty,
long life and good health
in the years to come.

Hon. D..A. Banks, O.J., C.D.
CHAIRMAN

to walk in the gardens with the corgis, spend time with members of her family and, as well as her meetings with her Private Secretary, receive the High Commissioner for Bangladesh and his wife, then a retiring member of her staff followed by the new Ambassador of the meeting the Sovereign has with her Prime Minister, and Mr Major will no doubt echo the opinion of all his predecessors that a Premier needs to be well briefed for the session. The Queen will be!

A day spent overseas, with HMY Britannia as base, provides a clear contrast,

Garden parties at Buckingham Palace are an annual fixture in the Royal calendar.

United States of America, who presented his letters of Credence. Next to be received were the British High Commissioner to Kenya, on whom the Queen conferred a Knighthood, Britain's new Ambassador to the Holy See, the Major-General Commanding Household Division, who was relinquishing his appointment and, finally, the Prime Minister. This was the routine weekly although again the boxes and the paperwork will receive their due attention. The day's programme will probably start with the Queen and the Duke of Edinburgh leaving the yacht soon before 10.00am in the morning. If it is not the first day of a State visit, which invariably includes observing the formalities customary in the host country and ending with a State Banquet given by the host, the programme will have been arranged to allow the Queen and the Duke, sometimes going on separate trips, to see as much of the country and its people as possible. Visits to schools and hospitals, factories and farms, business enterprises, receptions, lunch, one or two speeches — all could be in the programme with, in the the Queen, the boxes and for the Duke his own routine and on-going business.

At home a day's visit to a provincial town or city will keep the Queen and Prince Philip almost as busy as a day overseas. The programme will have been built around one major event, the opening of a new building

Relaxing on HMY Britannia, the Queen's floating palace when away from home.

evening, a visit to a concert or the theatre. It might, of course, be the occasion for the Queen and the Duke to entertain their hosts and if that is the case the Band of the Royal Marines, travelling with the royal party, will bring the day to a moving and impressive end by beating retreat. Whatever the programme it will have been a day on which the Queen and Prince Philip will have been out and about among the crowds for anything up to ten or twelve hours. Plus, for or of a bridge is a good example. Other engagements will be added and if it is, let us say, a visit to northern England or Wales, a two day programme may well be developed. It will inevitably allow the Queen and the Duke to meet as many people as possible but, as ever, allowing time for the official daily business. The fact that the Queen is Head of all three armed services and Supreme Governor of the Church of England (as well as having a special responsibility to the

Established Church of Scotland) is frequently recognised in the programmes arranged for such days.

Meetings of the Privy Council — the Queen summons ten such meetings a year on average — the series of investitures following the New Year and Birthday monarch was able to travel so widely and make contact with so many members of the general public and the Queen has taken full advantage of her opportunities to do so, her own circumstances make her unique it is true but they do not make her remote — almost any one of the days of

No previous monarch has ever travelled so widely and been seen by so many people.

Honours lists, incoming State visits, informal lunch parties, major receptions and sporting occasions like the Epsom Derby all have their place in the year's engagements, days which are regular but each in its own way different. The individuals involved make certain of that — the country is full of extraordinary characters, as the Queen is probably more aware than anyone else.

What almost all of these days will have had in common is that the Queen, usually with the Duke of Edinburgh, will have been meeting people. No previous the Queen's life will have made her further aware of the realities of the world most of us live in. Whether through the pomp and pageantry, grandeur and formality of so many of the national occasions or in far more relaxed situations the Queen works for and among her people. Many things have changed dramatically since 1952; the Queen's dedication to a life of service has not. The manner in which she has fulfilled the promise she made on her twenty first birthday is indeed typical of her.

A NEW ZEALAND TRIBUTE TO HER MAJESTY

The Directorate, Staff and Management of
The National Bank of New Zealand Limited
express their warmest good wishes to Her Majesty
Queen Elizabeth on this the 40th anniversary of
her accession to the throne.
For, and on behalf of, The National Bank
of New Zealand Limited.

J A Anderson
(Chief Executive Officer)

D H Tudhope C.M.G., D.F.C.
(Chairman)

The National Bank
of New Zealand Limited

A FAMILY OF NATIONS

"If history sees Victoria as the Queen who presided over the growth of the British Empire, it will surely see her great-great-grand-daughter Elizabeth II as the Queen who presided over decolonisation and the growth of the Commonwealth which replaced the Empire" says Commonwealth Secretary-General Chief Emeka Anyaoku.

Buckingham Palace is a natural focus of celebration in Britain for the 40th anniversary of the accession of Her Majesty The Queen. A little way off along the Mall, however, stands Marlborough House, a former royal residence, now the head-

Commonwealth. The Commonwealth, no less than Britain, is profoundly grateful for the inspirational quality of her leadership over those 40 years.

The anniversary of the accession will have been suitably marked in many parts of

During the Silver Jubilee Tour of 1977 the Queen opened Parliament in Wellington, New Zealand, one of the 17 independent sovereign countries where she is Head of State.

quarters of the Commonwealth Secretariat, which was established in 1965 to promote consultation and co-operation between Commonwealth governments. Its presence is a reminder that Queen Elizabeth II is not only monarch of the United Kingdom but also Head of the Commonwealth, a worldwide association of 50 independent sovereign nations, with a total population of roughly one and a half billion people. The 40th anniversary of the accession also marks 40 years of the Queen's role as Head of the

the Commonwealth on 6 February, and particularly, of course, in the other 16 independent sovereign countries where she is also Head of State. A second opportunity for commemoration in all Commonwealth countries — which include 28 republics and 5 national monarchies — offered itself very shortly afterwards on the second Monday in March, which since 1977 has been observed as Commonwealth Day. It is marked in Britain by a multifaith observance at Westminster Abbey, normally attended by the Queen as Head of the Commonwealth. A number of other multifaith observances are held, too, in other Commonwealth countries, and governments mark the occasion in differing ways. It is a day set aside for people throughout the Commonwealth, and

Opening the 32nd Commonwealth Parliamentary Conference in London in 1986.

especially young people in activities in their schools, to consider and celebrate the special qualities of the association and the many links which bind together its nations and peoples.

Commonwealth Heads of Government have been glad to make their own contri-bution to mark this 40th anniversary. They unanimously welcomed, at their 'retreat' at Victoria Falls during the Harare Summit, the Royal Anniversary Trust's proposal to present Her Majesty with a Commonwealth Mace bearing the flags and emblems of all member countries and decided to commemorate the occasion by commissioning a set of ceremonial gold goblets, one for each country, for use on major Commonwealth occasions in association with the Commonwealth mace.

The role of Head of the Commonwealth was affirmed when the modern, multiracial Commonwealth of equal sovereign states began to emerge after World War II. In 1947 India and Pakistan achieved independence, as did Ceylon (now Sri Lanka) in 1948, fundamentally altering the character of the former all-white Commonwealth consisting of Britain, Australia, Canada, New Zealand and at that time South Africa. India, led then by Prime Minister Jawaharlal Nehru, decided to become a republic thereby adopting her own constitutional Head of State. But India also sought continuing Commonwealth membership. After urgent consultations with the other seven Commonwealth

On the 1954 Royal Tour of Australia with J J Cahill, The Premier of New South Wales.

members, the London Declaration, adopted at the summit of April 1949, proffered to India the formula that was subsequently to be applied in all similar cases namely, India's 'acceptance of The King as the symbol of the free association of its independent member nations and as such the Head of the Commonwealth.'

Victoria as the Queen who presided over the growth of the British Empire, it will surely see her great-great-grand-daughter Elizabeth II as the Queen who presided over decolonisation and the growth of the Commonwealth which replaced the Empire.

Since the Queen has been Head of the Commonwealth for forty of the forty-three

The Royal Family has strong ties with Canada. The Queen Mother as well as the Queen is a regular visitor and Prince Andrew spent six months at college in Lakeland, Ontario.

This solution, typically for the Commonwealth, combined respect for constitutional forms with flexibility and pragmatism. Proof that it has worked is evinced by the Commonwealth's dramatic expansion: from the eight member countries at the time of the London Declaration to 50 today, including many countries in Africa, the Caribbean and the Pacific. The wisdom of Nehru, Attlee and their colleagues ensured the transformation of the Commonwealth into a dynamic, organically-developing association which was to become a force for good on the changed post-war international scene.

Given that Commonwealth membership is entirely voluntary and far from automatic, the growth of the modern Commonwealth is surely one of the most remarkable historical developments of our time. If history sees

years that the title and office have existed, it is true to say that she has defined the role by her practice. At the same time, in those four decades the Commonwealth has itself assumed its modern form as a vitally contemporary, forward-looking association of equal sovereign states and their peoples, located in every continent and ocean of the globe, which consult and co-operate in their own interests and those of the wider international community, and are dedicated collectively to the goals of freedom, democracy, international understanding, multiracialism and world peace.

The Queen's role as Head is now finely tuned in relation to the Commonwealth's needs. She has not only accommodated herself to the demands of a changing Commonwealth in a changing world but has also positively welcomed change. In doing

The Queen and the Royal Family have maintained close links with Australian life and in 1970 returned to join the celebrations marking James Cook's 'discovery' of Australia 200 years earlier.

Her Majesty the Queen
Buckingham Palace
The Mall
London SW1
England

Your Majesty,

On behalf of National Australia Bank Limited, sincere congratulations on the fortieth anniversary of Your Majesty's accession to the throne.

As a company based in Australia, but with substantial business links in the United Kingdom and Ireland, National Australia Bank is delighted to take part in this special tribute to the first 40 years of Your Majesty's reign.

Arguably, those 40 years have seen the most dramatic period of change in recorded history; but through all the change, Your Majesty's reign has shone like a beacon, a record of dedication, hard work and devotion to duty.

In Australia, despite the tyranny of distance, we have always felt close to Your Majesty. Our links to the Crown have constantly been renewed and strengthened by Your Majesty's frequent visits to our shores and by the visits of many members of the Royal Family.

Most recently, of course, Your Majesty's three-week visit in 1988 was a highlight of Australia's Bicentennial celebrations. It was a time when millions of Australians had the opportunity to greet Your Majesty, many of them on a personal basis.

Your Majesty, we bring greetings and warm best wishes from all members of the National Australia Bank Group in the UK and Ireland, which includes Clydesdale Bank PLC, Northern Bank Limited, Yorkshire Bank PLC and National Irish Bank; and National Australia Bank and its subsidiaries, branches and representative offices in 16 countries throughout the world.

Sir Rupert Clarke Bt MBE
Chairman

 Clydesdale Bank PLC

so, she has shown deep reservoirs of understanding, adaptability and commitment. But the personal qualities which Her Majesty has brought to the role go far beyond that. The Commonwealth has derived inspiration at all times from its Head because she shares and upholds its deepest principles, and embodies personally what is best about the

unseen attention to current events and personalities. I had reason to discover this personally when the Queen gave a reception in May 1974 for Commonwealth Senior Officials then meeting in London. I was assigned the pleasurable task of standing beside the Queen for an hour or more throughout the reception in order to

Whenever possible the Queen is present during the Commonwealth Heads of Government Meeting as she was in 1985 in Nassau, Bahamas.

association. A trader in a Zimbabwe market which she visited in 1991 put it simply but admirably in saying: 'You can see she has a good heart.' The leaders and peoples of all Commonwealth countries would, I am sure, endorse that observation unreservedly.

The continuity and stability which the Queen's Headship of 40 years has provided have made an outstanding contribution to the contemporary Commonwealth and the international standing which it enjoys today. She brings to her role a wisdom born of deep knowledge of the Commonwealth — its leaders, peoples, places, history and customs. She has served the Commonwealth longer by far than any of its national leaders have been at the helms of their countries. The knowledge of experience is constantly updated by assiduous even if

identify the officials — Cabinet Secretaries and the like — to her. I still recall with abiding admiration how she had something germane and knowledgeable to observe or inquire about all their countries.

The Commonwealth which she heads, and knows so well, is a complex and many-sided association. The biennial Commonwealth Heads of Government Meeting (or 'CHOGM' for short) is the apex of Commonwealth official consultation, below which are meetings of ministers in many key areas, and of officials and technical experts of all kinds, all serviced by the Commonwealth Secretariat established to promote intergovernmental consultation and co-operation, notably by acting on decisions taken at the summits. The Secretariat has its own multilateral technical assistance

Ghana became a member of the Commonwealth in 1957 and was visited by the Queen in 1961 when she toured West Africa with the Duke of Edinburgh.

programme, the Commonwealth Fund for Technical Co-operation (CFTC) set up in 1971 to supply to member states expertise and training in various fields of socio-economic development.

The Commonwealth also comprises networks of connections between the peoples of its countries. There are literally hundreds of Commonwealth non-governmental organisations (NGOs), some linking

When President Babangida visited Britain in 1989 it was the second State Visit by a Nigerian President during the Queen's reign.

Commemorative Coronation Stamp, 1953

*T*he Directors, Management and staff of NZI Insurance Limited congratulate Her Majesty the Queen on the 40th Anniversary of her accession to the throne.

NZI Insurance

 NZI Insurance New Zealand Limited
A member company of General Accident Group

DMB&B0941AT

The Queen and the Duke of Edinburgh visited Kiribati, formerly the Gilbert Islands, in 1982 during a tour of the Pacific Islands.

such professional groups as doctors, nurses, architects, lawyers and academics, others carrying out 'good works' for the blind, the disabled or the hungry, still others connecting sportsmen and hobbyists. There are also many Commonwealth clubs and societies in several member countries. All these help to ensure that Commonwealth ideas and principles reach down to the grassroots. Some of the activities in the non-governmental Commonwealth are nurtured by the Commonwealth Foundation, housed like the Secretariat at Marlborough House. The Queen has shared in and supported the activities of this 'people's Commonwealth' in many ways, from frequent attendances at the

Even as far away as we are, we've never been closer.

In a reign of 40 years Queen Elizabeth II has been dedicated to
strengthening the bonds between nations.
This commitment to bringing people together is one we share as
New Zealand's communication link to the world.

Telecom Corporation of New Zealand Limited

Commonwealth Games, to opening Commonwealth Parliamentary Conferences and other gatherings, and welcoming groups of visiting Commonwealth professionals to Buckingham Palace.

liberation movements, it was openly suggested in some quarters that the Queen should not go to Lusaka because of fears for her safety. Buckingham Palace took the unprecedented step of letting it be known

The Pacific islands of Tuvalu, formerly the Ellice Islands, became independent in 1978. The Queen visited the islands four years later in 1982.

The role of Head of this many-sided Commonwealth has been endowed with practical benefits by the Queen. An example is the role of the Queen at the biennial Commonwealth Heads of Government Meetings. While taking no part in the Meeting itself, she meets Heads of Government collectively at a banquet and gives separate audiences to each of the individual leaders. These private meetings, which are cherished by all, help to explain her unparalleled knowledge of the Commonwealth and the special relationship she enjoys with its political leaders. It goes without saying that the Queen has an influence on leaders and events which has enabled her to act as a focus for stability, reassurance and unity. That was clearly seen in early July 1979 prior to the Common-wealth's summit meeting in the Zambian capital of Lusaka. With the divisive intra-Commonwealth debate on how best to support Zimbabwe's struggle for indepen-dence at its height, and Zambia a base for both Zimbabwean and South African

that it remained Her Majesty's firm intention to go to Lusaka. Subsequently in Lusaka, The Queen's reception after her

The Queen first visited Jamaica in 1953 and was last there in 1983 for their 21st anniversary of independence.

banquet for all Heads of Government and the Secretary-General, which normally would have ended by 10.30pm, went on an hour or more longer.

The message was plain: for the Head of the Commonwealth it was business as usual, only more so. The Queen's coolness in the face of potential threats to the meeting, and the

The Loram Group

The Loram Group is pleased to extend sincere congratulations to Her Majesty Queen Elizabeth I on the 40th anniversary of her accession.

The Queen's devotion and dedication to duty are an inspiration to us all. As a figurehead with a true sense of commitment she is admired and respected worldwide. In everything she does she shows compassion, care and concern and works tirelessly to improve standards and set examples to all who meet and come in contact with her.

The Loram Group offers its enduring support and encouragement to Her Majesty in her leadership roles both globally, as Head of the Commonwealt and locally, as Colonel-in-Chief of the Calgary Highlanders.

The Loram Group is based in Calgary, Alberta, Canada, operating for its 94th year of business in international railroad maintenance, coal mining and oil and gas transportation, exploration and production

Photo Courtesy of The Calgary Herald

The Queen has visited the Solomon Islands twice during her reign, in 1974 and 1982.

human warmth and unity of purpose with which she imbued the occasion, contributed immeasurably to the success of that historic summit, which went on to lay the foundations for Zimbabwe's democratic independence and Commonwealth membership the following year. The Lusaka episode is typical of the way in which the Queen, in her role as Head of the Commonwealth, has sought to inspire and assist the association to overcome whatever divisions and disagreements occur, as they inevitably will from time to time.

Odaray Prospect – Deborah Lougheed Sinclair

STABILITY INTEGRITY HONOUR

During 40 years of committed service to the people of the United Kingdom and the Commonwealth, Her Royal Highness Queen Elizabeth II has expressed the highest values of responsibility and concern for all people.

Through the turbulence and change of the late Twentieth Century, the Queen has set a unique and exemplary standard for public conduct.

We at TransCanada PipeLines want to take this opportunity to offer our warmest congratulations, to express our heartfelt gratitude and to renew our own commitment to the service of our community.

Gerald J. Maier
President and Chief Executive Officer

On the occasion of the

40th Anniversary
of Her Majesty the Queen's
Accession to the Throne

TransCanada PipeLines

She has been just as much a force for stability and unity in her relationship with the peoples of the Commonwealth. Her concern to foster this relationship in several ways has been apparent. Through her Christmas and Commonwealth Day messages, no less than through her visits to every country of the Commonwealth, she regularly reaches out worldwide and performs what I consider to be one of her most valuable services to the Commonwealth, namely the promotion of the concept of common humanity. In her messages she has expressed, in language which has touched many hearts, the simple truths which are at the root of Commonwealth principles. She has called for compassion, understanding and human fellowship, in a world which has often been in dire need of these qualities, which she herself has exemplified.

In her messages and speeches, the Queen has conveyed the powerful conviction that the Commonwealth in all its aspects is something special in world affairs, with unique qualities of family feeling, friendliness and ease of understanding born of shared interests, principles and institutions

In 1977 the Queen experienced her first Concorde flight from Barbados. She returned there in 1989 to celebrate the 350th anniversary of their Parliament.

building on a common past.

As she pointed out when speaking at the Commonwealth Institute in London in 1987, the principles for which the Commonwealth stands 'are quite simply those which would, if universally applied, make the world a better place.' They are principles which Her Majesty Queen Elizabeth II, in her life of service to the Commonwealth as its Head, has never ceased to affirm and uphold.

PREMIERS
AND PREROGATIVES

John Major was only eight years old when the Queen came to the throne — The Prime Minister she inherited 40 years ago was the 77-year-old Winston Churchill. Lord Blake looks at the relationship between the monarch and her prime ministers.

Of all the pictures of the Queen's accession in February 1952, the photograph of that septuagenarian figure, Winston Churchill, waiting bareheaded on the tarmac at London Airport to receive the young Sovereign as she came down the plane steps after her flight back from Kenya, was to be long remembered.

Churchill was the first of the nine Prime Ministers there have been since then. The Queen had inherited him: his second term of office had begun in October 1951, a few months before her father died. The relationship between minister and monarch was almost a love affair on his side. Audiences at the palace became longer and longer, reminding one of Melbourne and Queen Victoria. Three years later in April 1955 Churchill at last bowed out at the age of eighty. What honour would be appropriate for a man who on any view stood out as one of the greatest statesmen in British history?

This was a decision for the Queen. It is sometimes said that the only honours she can confer otherwise than 'on advice' are the Garter, the Order of Merit and the various grades of the Royal Victorian Order. This is generally true, but there is another category — the peerage traditionally conferred on a resigning Prime Minister. In

John Major, the ninth Prime Minister of the current reign.

1957 the Queen offered an earldom to Anthony Eden without taking 'advice', and in 1963 told Harold Macmillan that 'I could have one **'on her authority'** (that is not "on advice") if ever I wanted it. This was very gracious'.[1] But the customary earldom would not do for Churchill. His private secretary, Sir John Colville, suggested a dukedom, but he was told that a decision had been made — no more dukes outside the royal family. The Queen would like to make the offer, if it was certain that Churchill would refuse. When the matter was raised in confidence with him he said he would under no circumstances accept. Yet at his resignation interview he apparently paused when the offer was made. 'I very nearly accepted,' he said, but he stuck to his determination to die as Winston Churchill. 'I asked her to forgive my not accepting it. And, do you know, it's an odd thing, but she seemed almost relieved'.[2]

The remaining eight Prime Ministers were formally appointed by her. Prime Ministers are neither elected by Parliament nor by 'the people'. Constitutionally they are royal nominees but no Prime Minister could nowadays carry on, as the younger Pitt did for some months in 1784, without a Parliamentary majority and relying on royal support. A modern Prime Minister must command a majority in the House of Commons, though he need not be a party leader. Lloyd George never was. MacDonald from 1931 to 1935 led no party. Churchill in a few months in 1940 was in the same position. Those situations were abnormal. In

Harold Macmillan who succeeded Anthony Eden as Prime Minister in 1957.

the Queen's reign every Prime Minister has been leader of the party which possesses a majority in the House of Commons. This is invariably the position today, and there is only one appointment that the Queen can make. Since 1965 the Conservatives have had an intra-party electoral system, and in 1957 Labour had made it clear that no member would be expected to accept the premiership unless he had first been elected leader of the Parliamentary party.

In the first dozen years of the Queen's reign the Conservatives were in power, but, oddly perhaps, had never devised an electoral system for the leadership in the event of a Prime Minister resigning — or dying — in the mid term of a parliament. To do so seems to have been regarded as an infringement of the royal prerogative. There was no problem when Churchill resigned. Eden was universally regarded as the inevitable successor. It was a different matter when Eden resigned in January 1957. There were two powerful candidates, Harold

Macmillan and 'Rab' Butler. Either, if appointed, would have commanded the support of their party and of a majority in the House. The natural course for the monarch in such circumstances was to ask for the view of the outgoing Prime Minister. He was not bound to give it nor she to take it, for it could not be 'binding advice' in the constitutional sense. If not 'binding' it was certain to be persuasive. But Eden, for whatever reason, though asked for his recommendation, was not willing to give it. Instead he suggested that she should consult a senior figure in the Cabinet, who could not himself be a runner, the obvious name being Lord Salisbury.

In partnership with the Lord Chancellor, Salisbury polled the Cabinet one by one lisping 'Well, which is it, Wab or Hawold'. The almost unanimous answer was Macmillan, reinforced by Churchill independently consulted, and by a few soundings among other party panjandrums. Supporters of Butler were angry. A conspiracy

Anthony Eden who served as Prime Minister from 1955 - 1957.

from Hatfield was alleged and Salisbury was ridiculously dubbed as 'the King Maker'. In fact the result was almost certainly the same as if there had been a party election, and no one criticised the Queen.

FARSONS

*Mr. Lewis V. Farrugia A.&C.E., O.B.E., President of the
Chamber of Commerce, welcoming H.R.H. Princess Elizabeth at
the opening of an Industrial Exhibition marking the First
Centenary of the Chamber. November 1949, Valletta, Malta.*

It is an honour and a privilege to pay tribute to H.M. Queen Elizabeth II on the occasion of the 40th Anniversary of her Accession to the British throne.

Over 40 years ago the young 21-year-old Princess pledged herself to her country and her people with the words 'I declare before you that my whole life whether it be long or short shall be devoted to your service . . . .' Those words have proved to be the yardstick by which she has ruled over the last four decades.

We in Malta will always remember H.M. The Queen and H.R.H. Prince Philip with affection and warmth particularly given that, as a young married couple, they spent two years living here where the Prince was stationed as a Royal Naval Officer.

They, as well as other members of the Royal Family have returned regularly. Most recently the Duke of Edinburgh joined in the 25th anniversary celebrations of Malta's independence in 1989. We are looking forward with anticipation to Her Majesty's visit in May 1992.

The Maltese people wish H.M. Queen Elizabeth II many more years of peaceful reign.

Anthony Miceli Farrugia, K.M., K.L.J.
Chairman

Winston Churchill, the first of the Queen's Prime Ministers, who was offered, but declined, a dukedom when he resigned in 1955.

The second and last occasion involving the royal prerogative was more controversial. In October 1963 Macmillan resigned — unnecessarily as it turned out — from a prostate malady far less serious than he was led to believe. It was an awkward moment, the eve of the Conservative Party Conference in Blackpool. On his post-operational sick bed he was given to understand that the Palace would like his

James Callaghan was the first Prime Minister to succeed to the post as a result of a party election.

advice. He did not hesitate to give it in favour of Lord Home, in preference to Rab Butler and Lord Hailsham after complicated second hand enquiries about Conservative sentiment. Some of the answers have been disputed ever since, but no one could fault the Queen for taking his advice, once she had asked for it.

Doubts about the so-called 'Magic Circle', that allegedly engineered the succession resulted in 1965 in the adoption of an electoral system for the Conservative leadership. It was under this that Edward Heath was chosen Leader in 1965 and, under a revised version, Margaret Thatcher ten years later. Neither was in office at the time, and so the Queen was not affected. But in 1976 for the first time a party election produced a Prime

Minister, James Callaghan to succeed Harold Wilson who had resigned. In November 1990 the same process again produced a new Prime Minister, John Major in place of Margaret Thatcher. The Queen was in each case bound to appoint the elected leader, and, save in very exceptional circumstances this must be the future pattern. The problems of 1957 and 1963 are now a part of history.

There has often been media gossip about possible dissension between Buckingham Palace and 10 Downing Street. What did she really think about Suez? Did she, as alleged by a jet-lagged and soon dismissed press secretary, dislike certain aspects of Thatcherism? Did she regard some of her Prime Ministers as unduly luke warm about the Commonwealth? Did she haul Margaret Thatcher over the coals after President Reagan invaded Grenada? The answer is that no one knows. Such guesses are pure speculation. The weekly interview with the

Margaret Thatcher, the first female British Prime Minister.

Prime Minister is a matter of extreme confidentiality. There is no one else present, and there is no agenda. Even in this era of endless 'leaks' no breach of confidence has ever occurred. Being human the Queen may have her opinions about affairs of state and she may prefer the conversation and company of some Prime Ministers to others. But she has never stepped beyond the bounds of political his mind'. Whether the Queen ever has warned a Prime Minister or — more likely — hinted at doubts or misgivings about a certain course of action, only she and the relevant Minister can know. But if she has

The 250th anniversary of Downing Street as the home of the British prime minister saw the Queen join six of her Prime Ministers to celebrate the occasion.

impartiality, and, to judge from such letters as have been published, her relations with successive Prime Ministers have been cordial, sympathetic and supportive. Whether she has recorded her private opinions, as Queen Victoria did in letters of much vigour to her secretary, Sir Henry Ponsonby, one does not know. If so they will certainly not be published in her lifetime.

The Queen's right to appoint a Prime Minister is restricted; her right to dismiss him is obsolete; her right to refuse him a dissolution is only usable in extraordinary circumstances. But she undoubtedly still possesses the rights enumerated by Bagehot in his famous English Constitution (1867): 'the right to be consulted, the right to encourage and the right to warn'. Of the latter Bagehot observes that an articulate Monarch who exercised it 'could not help moving his Minister. He might not always turn his course but he would always trouble

one can safely say that only a very obdurate or self-willed Prime Minister would fail to pay attention and to argue his case with as much clarity and cogency as he can muster. Apart from the instinctive respect which any First Minister of the Crown feels for the actual wearer, there is her experience of forty years and nine Prime Ministers, especially now that a new generation is coming to the fore in politics. John Major was only eight when she succeeded to the throne, and Neil Kinnock was nine. She can personally remember episodes which to them are at best items in a history book that they read at school. One can only hope that this wealth of experience will long be available to successive future Prime Ministers.

[1] Harold Macmillan, **The End of the Day** (1973), 518
[2] Martin Gilbert, **Never Despair, Churchill 1945-65** (1988) 1124

We join our colleagues from the best of British Industry in congratulating Her Majesty on the 40th Anniversary of her Accession.

Strengths that fit together

Golden Wonder
Spillers Foods
Homepride
Lucas Ingredients
Spillers Milling
Martin-Brower
Dalgety Agriculture
Pig Improvement Company

DALGETY

100 George Street London W1H 5RH

BY ROYAL
APPOINTMENT

The Royal Warrant Holders Association reflects the range of services offered to the Royal Family and is a coveted badge of distinction in the commercial world. Commander Faulkner, Secretary of The Association since 1979, explains its origins and organisation.

The 13th Supplement to The London Gazette, published by Her Majesty's Stationery Office on 31st December 1991 listed over 800 firms privileged to hold a Royal Warrant of Appointment. Only four Mother, 42 by The Duke of Edinburgh and, The Prince of Wales, who has only been granting his Royal Warrant since July 1981, some 122.

Study the list more carefully and it

British monarchy has had a long standing love of horses. The saddler to the Queen is Michael Gidden of W and H Gidden Ltd.

members of the Royal Household currently grant this honour — HM The Queen, HRH The Duke of Edinburgh, HM Queen Elizabeth The Queen Mother and HRH The Prince of Wales. Of the 1,133 Royal Warrants listed some 743 have been granted by HM The Queen, 226 by HM The Queen becomes apparent that no professional names occur. This is simply because all Royal Warrant holders are tradesmen; professional business men are ineligible. No banks, solicitors, doctors or insurance companies will appear on the list, or ever have done.

Some names appear in more than one list as a selective number hold more than one Royal Warrant. Indeed, a small minority, for example Harrods, Hatchards and Sycamore Laundry hold all four Royal Warrants.

Royal Warrants can be held by individuals as well as companies, the names include both manufacturers and retailers, large and small.

Household, although that is indeed the first step. It is only after a three year period of consistent and substantial supply that a firm, if it so wishes, can apply for a Royal Warrant of Appointment to the Grantor whose household the firm has been supplying.

For example, a firm might supply fish on a regular basis to The Queen's Household.

A small minority of Warrant Holders hold all four Warrants.

Inevitably, the largest concentration of Royal Warrant Holders is found in London but the location of out of town Royal residences can be spotted by the number of Royal Warrant Holders in Windsor, Kings Lynn, Ballater and Edinburgh. But the geographical location is widespread not just throughout Britain but worldwide. Royal Warrant Holders can be found in Kirkwall, where the suppliers of honey are based as well as in France, the home of the producers of champagne, and on the other side of the world where an Australian jeweller holds the Queen's Warrant for a cup presented each year to the winner of a horse race.

How does a firm get a Royal Warrant? Not simply by supplying goods to a Royal

Three years from the date of the first supply 'Mr Fish & Co' complete an application form which is sent to The Royal Household Tradesmens Warrants Committee. This Committee meets once a year and, based on the quality of the goods and service given, will make a recommendation that 'Mr Fish & Co' be considered. This recommendation will then be placed before Her Majesty, who makes the final decision to grant her Royal Warrant.

If 'Mr Fish & Co' is fortunate enough to be granted the Queen's Royal Warrant he will be sent his Royal Warrant of Appointment, which is signed by The Lord Chamberlain. This states that "by command of The Queen the firm of Mr Fish & Co has been appointed in to the

Eric Lobb of Lobb's the shoemaker, holders of three Royal Warrants, where it takes six separate craftsmen to make a pair of shoes or boots.

THE FUTURE IS L👓KING GOOD

All the employees within the Dollond & Aitchison

Group congratulate Her Majesty Queen Elizabeth II

on the 40th Anniversary of an historic reign.

When our company was established in the year 1750,

King George II was on the throne.

During those 241 years Dollond & Aitchison has

developed substantially whilst changing with the needs

of society to be the NUMBER ONE NAME IN SIGHT

in Europe through the provision of professional

eyecare and consumer choice:

- Market leader in five countries
- Focus on serving Europe
- Dedicated to "Excellence in Sight"

We are proud and confident in following the high

standards and examples, always set by Her Majesty,

to achieve our exciting strategic developments within

Europe in the years ahead.

DOLLOND & AITCHISON

ESTABLISHED 1750

Makers of optical history.
Guardians of great traditions.

place and quality of fishmonger to Her Majesty and that the Warrant is granted to 'Mr John Smith'. Although a company may be granted the honour, it is an individual, known as the Grantee, within that company who is granted the Royal Warrant and who holds it on behalf of the company. This individual is responsible for ensuring that the rules in connection with the use of The Royal Arms are observed.

The firm may now use their newly acquired honour in specific controlled circumstances. They are allowed to display The Royal Arms, supported at all times by their legend. For example, 'By Appointment to HM The Queen. Fishmongers. Mr Fish & Co, London'. This legend can also appear on stationery and advertising matter as well as outside the company premises and on commercial vehicles.

A firm granted the Royal Warrant which also manufactures the item concerned has the right to carry the Royal Warrant on the item and/or its packaging as appropriate. This can be found on a wide range of goods from clothing to cornflakes.

A Royal Warrant is reviewed every ten years. Providing a company is still supplying quality goods and services, they have a strong chance of the Warrant being renewed for a further period of ten years. But firms can lose their Royal Warrants. The Warrant is non-transferable and a company going out of business, being sold on or amalgamated with another would have their Warrant cancelled. If the company changes character or if a serious breach of rules occurs the Warrant would also be cancelled.

Warrant Holders are not allowed to reveal details of the services they give to a Royal Household, neither can they contribute to any article concerning the Queen or the Royal Family. This is why Warrant Holders are never prepared to discuss their Royal Warrant with either the Press or anyone who might breach their code of confidentiality.

Royal Warrants date back as far as the 12th century when trades and crafts obtained their first formal links with the Crown in a collective manner by means of Royal Charters to their respective Guilds. These Guilds later became know as Livery Companies, owing to the distinctive dress (livery) worn by their Freemen.

The very first Royal Charter dates from 1155 when Henry II bestowed his Royal Patronage on the Weavers Company. The Royal Warrant of Appointment which conferred individual, as opposed to collective, patronage was a natural follow on from the Royal Charter. It is not known exactly when the first Royal Warrant of Appointment was granted, but it is believed that Queen Elizabeth I was the first to do so and it is certain that Charles II extended the practice. Royal Warrant Holders are still in existence today whose first Warrant dates back to the 18th century. These include the piano manufacturers, Broadwood, and the outfitters, Threshers and Glenny.

David Coward, Royal brushmaker, with some of his raw materials and finished products.

In the reign of Henry VIII, the Statues of Eltham, drawn up for the "good order of his household", a Mr Thomas Hewytt was appointed "to serve the court with Swannes and Cranes, and all kinds of wildfoul, in every degree according to the articles specified." And Anne Harris was appointed the King's Laundresse and received £1 a year "for the washing of the napery which shall serve the King's Own Table".

In 1684, *The Present State of England*, a periodical volume produced by a Doctor at

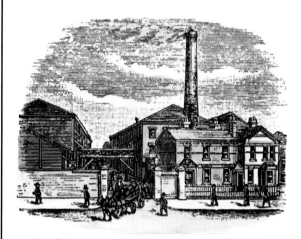

Law, Edward Chamberlayne, lists several names of suppliers of goods and services. These include a Haberdasher of Hats, Button Maker, Sword Cutter and even an Operator for the Teeth and a Corn Cutter. It also includes a Golf-club Maker, not surprising considering that James I first introduced the game of golf to England.

Twinings and Walls can be found in this group.

Interestingly, Queen Victoria was one of the first to award Warrants to women — in 1861 there were about a dozen women Grantees. Today, there are over twenty-five women holding a Royal Warrant.

The Royal Warrant of Appointment to

Lang Brothers Limited distillery at Glengoyne near Loch Lomond. They hold the Queen Mother's Warrant.

However it was during the reign of Queen Victoria that The Royal Warrant reached its present scale in size and organisation. The rapid growth and diversity of manufacturers, higher standards of living and the creation of new needs, brought about a greater and more varied expenditure from the Royal Treasury. There are still some twenty-six Royal Warrant Holders who have held the Royal Warrant continuously since Queen Victoria first granted her Royal Warrant in 1837. Well known names such as Cadbury, Garrards, Justerini & Brooks, Minton, Purdey, Schweppes,

tradesmen is still considered the 'blue riband' of the commercial world. The most recent list reflects the range of services offered to the Royal Family, from the more everyday services of food, drink and clothing through to technology and machinery. But whatever the service or goods supplied all the holders are honoured with their coveted distinction which is rightly considered as a badge of distinction as well as a guarantee of the integrity of the firm, the excellence of its products and, above all, a signal honour bestowed on them by their Queen or Prince for services rendered.

TRADITION AND HERITAGE

sought after by many - achieved by few

We congratulate
Her Majesty Queen Elizabeth II on the
40th anniversary of her accession
to the throne and offer our best wishes
for the future.

The Natural Name for Knitwear
since 1815

REWARDS FOR EXCELLENCE

John Smith, Head of The Queen's Award office, looks at the twenty-seven year history of The Queen's Awards, one of the most prestigious accolades in the commercial world.

The Queen's Awards Scheme was introduced in 1965 when business and industry were about to enter an era which would encompass — as described by the then Prime Minister, Harold Wilson, — "the white heat of the technological revolution."

They were instituted by Royal Warrant in accordance with the recommendations of a committee chaired by HRH The Duke of Edinburgh and since their inception more than 3,000 companies have been recipients.

Two crucial factors in the nation's economy are export performance and technological achievement and the Awards were introduced to recognise excellence in those fields.

The Queen's Awards are the highest corporate honour that can be bestowed on UK companies and they reflect the vast range of innovative marketing and technical skills which help keep those companies in the vanguard of competitive worldwide markets.

In the first decade of the Awards, originally known as the Queen's Award to Industry, the winner received a single Award for export or technological achievement or a combination of both.

Since 1975, two distinct separate Awards have been granted: The Queen's Award for Export Achievement and The Queen's Award for Technological Achievement.

A third award has now been added. The Prime Minister announced in the House of Commons in January this year that the Queen had given her approval in principle to the introduction of The Queen's Award for Environmental Achievement.

The new award will recognise product and process development which has major benefits for the environment and which is commercially successful. Applications will be sought in the summer this year and the first winners will be announced in 1993.

The Queen's Awards are made by the Queen on the advice of the Prime Minister, who is assisted by an Advisory Committee which includes representatives of government, industry, commerce and trade unions. They are announced annually on 21 April — the Queen's birthday.

In welcoming the 1991 Awards the Prince of Wales noted that in his endeavours to encourage British innovation, UK companies could not hope to prosper in the long term if they limited their horizons to the domestic marketplace.

Not only were there greatly expanded sales opportunities abroad but companies would have a much better chance of keeping a sharp competitive edge if it were honed continuously against the range of products and services available internationally.

At the same time Prime Minister John Major commented: "I have a particular regard for the Queen's Awards. They recognise the dedication and support of all employees throughout a successful firm. In addition, they do not discriminate in terms of size. The small enterprise is judged on an equal footing with the big corporation.

"It is apt that the Queen's Awards honour achievement in the fields of export and technology. These are both essential to the growth of the country's economy and to our international reputation for competitiveness. The winners are doing our country a vital service.

trum of industry manufacturing, consumer goods, engineering, service industries and 'invisibles' such as banking, insurance and hotels, to name but a few.

Among the goods and services produced by the 1991 winners were laminated glass fibre trays; cryogenic plant and equipment; cashmere garments; liquid cooled thyristor

Ralph Hodge, Chief Executive of ICI Chemicals & Polymers Ltd, receives The Queen's Award for Technological Achievement for the development of a revolutionary system for the purification of liquids and gases.

"Flying the Queen's Award flag and displaying the emblem is a proud and clear signal to customers and competitors, both at home and abroad that companies have reached the pinnacle of excellence."

Unlike personal honours, the Queen's Awards must be applied for — indeed it is only through application that companies can win. Any UK company can apply. Companies which operate as a 'unit' of the UK economy, as well as UK subsidiaries of foreign companies, are eligible. Applications are not accepted from individuals, but sole-proprietorships with any number of employees, partnerships of two people and identifiable 'divisions' of companies can apply.

Awards are granted across a broad spec-

valves; insects and mites; orthopaedic implants; marmalade and smoked salmon.

Take, for example, the JEM Smoke Machine Co. Ltd. in Spilsby, Lincolnshire which won an Export Award in 1991.

Founded in 1980, quickly established itself as a leading manufacturer of smoke generating and special effects equipment as well as a range of non-toxic water based smoke and fog fluids which were approved worldwide on their health and safety factors.

From initial discotheque installations the company's products were soon in demand for special effects in the theatre, film and television industries.

JEM products are not restricted to the artistic field. Fire fighting authorities worldwide train in smoke filled buildings

A HISTORY OF INNOVATION AND SERVICE

Rover Group is proud to join the nation – and the world – in paying tribute to Her Majesty Queen Elizabeth II on the occasion of the Fortieth Anniversary of her accession and expressing great pride in her achievements.

As the major British car manufacturer, we shall always strive to develop products which represent the best of British vehicle design and engineering excellence across the world.

Rover believes that its commitment to produce excellence should be matched by its determination to contribute – environmentally and socially – to the community from which it draws its business. Environmentally compatible manufacturing methods, designs for re-cycling, the use of environmentally sound materials – these are key elements in its product development process.

Rover's Education Partnership Programme has progressively forged an innovative relationship with local schools, fostering understanding and a lifetime commitment to learning. The company also actively pursues opportunities to educate the public into safer and more secure driving habits.

These activities – and a great deal more – ensure Rover not only makes a vital contribution to the economy, but to community life as a whole.

**HER MAJESTY THE QUEEN'S
40TH ANNIVERSARY**

LICENSED BY CELEBRATION 1992 LIMITED

John Towers
JOHN TOWERS
Group Managing Director

ROVER GROUP

RAISING STANDARDS

HER MAJESTY QUEEN ELIZABETH II has combined her own open and accessible style with the most professional approach to her duties.

During her reign, computer technology has evolved to influence almost every aspect of business and leisure. Logica has emerged as the largest independent computer systems and consultancy company headquartered in the UK.

Our success stems from our commitment to achieving the highest standards of quality work, and the effective application of information technology through close relationships with our clients worldwide.

We are proud to stand for the best traditions of the UK in professionalism, innovation and excellence.

Logica plc 68 Newman Street, London W1A 4SE
Telephone +44 71 637 9111 Fax +44 71 637 822

using continuous output smoke machines. Security firms use JEM machines to fill bank vaults with smoke when intrudents are detected and the aerospace industries use JEM smoke in wind tunnels for visually monitoring airflow over aircraft wings.

Other clients include foreign naval and air force establishments which use the equipment for training purposed.

In order to be considered for an Export Award applicants are judged on three years' performance and must demonstrate "a substantial and sustained increase in export earnings to a level which is outstanding for the products or services concerned and for the size of the applicant unit's operations. In addition, established exporters, who have a consistently high export performance but are unable to demonstrate dramatic export growth over three years, can have earlier export achievements taken into account. Consideration is given only to export orders which have been fulfilled — undelivered orders and estimates are ignored."

Those seeking a Technological Achievement Award must show "a significant advance, leading to increased efficiency, in the application of technology to a production or development process in British industry or the production for sale of goods which incorporate new and advanced technological qualities."

Innovation by itself, however is not enough. Since a principal aim of this award is to counteract the impression that Britain, despite winning many Nobel prizes for natural inventiveness, often fails to exploit it, applicants must also provide evidence of a product's commercial success.

Those seeking the Environment Award will be expected to show a significant advance in the development of products, technology or processes which offer benefits in environmental terms and which are commercially successful.

An award is held for five years and entitles the holder to fly the Awards flag and winning companies can display the Emblem, in a variety of ways — on letterheading, products and on personal items.

The prestige of winning an Award can give a company a much higher profile, open doors and bring with it a number of beneficial spin-offs. Not least amongst these can be a more amenable bank manager and an increase in business. Overseas companies, for example, see a firm which has received such formal royal and governmental recognition, as one that can be relied on for quality and initiative.

Following the announcement of the winners in the London Gazette a presentation is made to each company by the Queen's representative, the Lord Lieutenant of the County (or the Lord Major in the City of London). This is usually carried out on a company's premises so that all those involved with the company, who have contributed towards the work which has resulted in the Award, can join the celebrations. The Award — set in metal within a polished block — is presented to

Dr John Ley and Sir Ashley Ponsonby with Coates Coatings Ltd Award for Export Achievement

the company together with a Grant of Appointment containing the signatures of the Queen and the Prime Minister.

In addition, three representatives from each winning firm are normally invited to attend a reception at Buckingham Palace, hosted by the Queen and other members of the Royal Family.

Clearly this 'corporate honour' is much sought after by many excellent firms and organisations in Britain. All the applicants are in fact 'winners' in that they have successfully exploited their export potential or their technological advantage in the market place. From these are selected, after careful scrutiny and assessment, the outstanding performers.

Our congratulations

A FAMILY CONCERN

The Royal Family support many causes and organisations as individuals, veering towards their own personal interests and concerns. But on matters of the environment and conservation they have joined together to give their support. Miranda Barrington reports.

With the recent announcement that the Queen's Award to Industry will now include an award for Environmental Achievement, it could be thought that the Royal seal of approval has finally been given to environmental concerns. No longer just the priority of a slightly eccentric Prince known for his intimate conversations with plants, but an acceptable and worthwhile cause.

The Queen's Award will no doubt strengthen the cause but, in fact, the Royal Family have been staunch supporters for many years of the need to look after the planet on which we live. Whether through the conservation of endangered species or concern for the environment, members of the Royal Family have been speaking out on the issue of years.

None more so than Prince Philip, the Duke of Edinburgh, who was well ahead of his time when as UK President of the World Wildlife Fund he stated bluntly that 'If nature does not survive, neither will man'. It is now over thirty years since the Prince first spoke on the issue, when green was a colour and

The launch of the campaign for lead free petrol was held in the Royal Mews.

nothing more. His comments were not taken as seriously then as his son's comments are taken today, now that 'Green' issues have become fashionable.

However, being unfashionable or controversial has never stopped Prince Philip speaking his mind. He has followed and spoken out on global conservation issues for many years. As International President of the World Wide Fund for Nature his high profile role has given him an ideal platform from which to publicise the conservation of endangered species. But he has also spoken as strongly on issues of exploitation of soil and vegetation as well as the population explosion. He expresses his views clearly and simply with the knowledge and foresight of someone who has travelled the world and seen many of the problems first hand.

"The point is that this planet sustains life because there is life on this planet. It is this life that sustains the atmosphere.

"If we change the biological balance, we may well create a new atmosphere, one which may prevent life from surviving. We could become like one of those planets that does not support life at all. That may sound a bit violent but we have already discovered, after a long period of development, the pollution of the atmosphere by what is known as acid rain.

"This is now beginning to have an effect on the growth of trees in forests. Forests are the basic producers of oxygen.

put by for the next year, crops must be rotated if soil is not to be exhausted and animal stocks kept healthy and preserved for breeding. Sophisticated though the world might be, it is the basic cycle of nature that keeps the planet healthy and once an imbalance occurs the planet becomes a less and less healthy place to live.

The Prince has taken that basic

Prince Charles has worked hard to bring his concern for the environment into the public eye.

"If we destroy our forests, we are going to seriously affect the recycling of carbon dioxide which produces our supply of oxygen — in which case our whole life-support system will gradually run down."

This sounds like Prince Charles but it was, in fact, his father speaking in an interview in 1985. An argument built on common sense and a passionate concern for global issues.

Growing up in the countryside gave Prince Philip the foundation for his beliefs today. Simple farming methods form the basis of conservation. Enough seed must be

upbringing and can argue clearly and logically on the need for conservation in its broadest sense. And he has not been shy in speaking out. In 1988 he was criticised for attacking world governments for their "obsession with economic growth which has succeeded in destroying whatever pretension man ever had to being a special creation with special responsibilities for the rest of creation."

In a private audience with The Pope in June 1990 he stressed that population growth was at the root of the environmental crisis. This visit was part of a broader

Highgrove House, home of the Prince and Princess of Wales, boasts a beautiful wildflower border.

Wholly committed to a cleaner environment

We congratulate Her Majesty the Queen on the 40th anniversary of her Accession to the throne.

Arjo Wiggins Appleton

the new name in paper

campaign which he said was "trying to get the religions to address their relationship with nature". As a result leaders of seven faiths have agreed to work with the World Wide Fund for Nature in spreading the message of conservation .The Prince has stressed on many occasions the fact that there is a limit to the availability of basic

through Thailand, Singapore, Indonesia, East Malaysia, Brunei, Darusalam, and Bahrain. At every stop he spoke to government leaders and businessmen urging them to make every effort to conserve the environment.

The relationship between Prince Charles and his father has been the subject of much debate, but of one thing there is no doubt

Prince Philip, like other members of his family, practises what he preaches — including driving an electric car.

goods on the planet and the more people there are, the greater the demand.

Prince Philip has often, and wrongly, been seen merely as the consort dutifully trailing behind his wife. This is far from true. Whenever possible, and particularly on overseas tours, the Prince often leaves the Queen to involve himself in his own particular projects. From the early planning stages of a tour he will suggest additions and changes to itineraries because his personal knowledge of local conditions allow him to make suggestions to improve the schedules drawn up. And it also allows him to visit projects or speak to individuals or organisations first-hand.

In 1989 he attended the Commonwealth Heads of Government Meeting in Kuala Lumpur. As soon as the formal part of the visit had been concluded, Prince Philip left his wife for his own extended tour. This took him

— that they are in complete agreement on the subjects of conservation and environmental issues.

When the Duke first spoke out on the subject, he was indulged but largely ignored, when Prince Charles first spoke out some twenty years ago, he was labelled a crank.

But the Prince of Wales has served his apprenticeship, done his homework and has a unique network of contacts. He has learned his subject well and, more importantly, is passionate in his beliefs. His most spectacular successes have been through the Prince of Wales Business Leaders Forum.

The Royal Family have always worked hard whenever possible in a high powered public relations role promoting Great Britain and in particular, British industry. Through meeting industrialists worldwide Prince Charles became more ambitious in his goals and recognised that

CONSISTENT VALUES IN AN EVER CHANGING WORLD

Safe stewardship is the key to our future, as a nation, as individuals, and over the last forty years we have had this through the remarkable leadership of Her Majesty the Queen who has provided constancy and inspiration.

Friends Provident has sustained a commitment to helping millions of people look forward to a better future. This is typified by our Stewardship Funds, investment opportunities which seek to conserve the world's natural resources, not to abuse them, nor exploit its animals or peoples.

Our Stewardship range offers people the chance to prosper by investing in a better world - a sentiment that must surely last, regardless of all other changes.

Friends Provident is the business name of the Friends Provident Marketing
Group, members of which are members of Lautro and/or IMRO.

Prince Philip first spoke out on the need to look after the planet and its inhabitants over thirty years ago.

international business could be, if used correctly, a powerful agent for change. Moreover, economic goals were not enough. If businesses were to be truly successful they had to assume social responsibilities.

The Business Leaders Forum presents major corporations with commercially attractive packages. The Prince works had

through the Forum to illustrate and educate, showing industrialists that economic success and social responsibility can be compatible. Early in 1990 one hundred of the world's top executive from 13 countries accepted an invitation from the Prince of Wales to attend a Business Leaders Forum in Charleston, South Carolina, USA. This

TENGELMANN
Group of Firms

Congratulations to Her Majesty

The Haub family and the great number of people who work in the TENGELMANN Group's widespread grocery chains throughout Germany, send a hearty salute to Her Majesty Queen Elizabeth the Second on the occasion of the 40th anniversary of her Accession.

Our congratulations are all the warmer because, as pioneers ourselves of practical regulations to fight industrial pollution of the earth's atmosphere, we have long watched with admiration the special encouragement given by the British Head of State and her Royal Family to the crusades for a purer environment.

Our own "environmentally friendly" marketing policies which are mandatory in all our stores, began well over twenty years ago. In fact, it was my mother, Elisabeth Haub, who instigated TENGELMANN's activities for the sake of our environment, and our family-owned company is proud to be recognised as t h e Environment Protectors among the food retailers in Germany.

May Your Majesty's sovereignty and good health long continue, matched by a cleaner, greener world surrounding us all.

Erivan Haub

Erivan Haub

Chairman and CEO
Owner
The TENGELMANN Group

Unternehmensgruppe TENGELMANN · Wissollstraße 5-43 · 4330 Mülheim an der Ruhr · Germany

forum provided an environment for the executives of multi-national companies to learn first hand that good corporate citizenship could also be good business.

The Forum is not just a round of dinners and speeches. It presents programmes designed to make people look at what they are doing to, and for, the environments in which their companies are based, on a national and international level.

And these forums are not just meetings, they are springboards. Three months after the Charleston meeting, the Prince of Wales invited Western executives to Hungary which resulted in many privately funded projects being started to create employment. These projects are run and controlled by local people but the Business Leaders Forum will act as a "corporate ambassador" showing by example how corporate citizenship can work. Small projects today, but in five years time they could well be the catalyst for much larger business in Eastern Europe.

Business Leaders Forum meetings take place regularly around the world attracting the most influential executives from major corporations. The Prince has used his unique position to galvanise support and change from the highest level. And the number of companies who are now including corporate responsibility into their criteria shows how successful he has been.

The Prince of Wales has been criticised for stepping outside the boundaries which normally surround members of the Royal Family. Like children, they should be seen and not heard. The Prince has never been content to accept a passive role knowing that when he speaks out his words will have worldwide impact.

In March 1991 at the conference "What On Earth is to be Done", organised by the International Institute for Environment and Development, he warned of the dangers of expecting progress to go on making the world more comfortable and technology to solve problems. He stressed the importance of tackling the root causes of the problems before it was too late. "It is my belief that until more people concentrate on development which meets basic human needs, combined with enlightened stewardship of nature's capital, human and environmental tragedies will continue to unfold", he said.

He stressed that the true test of a civilised society was its commitment to tackling poverty, hunger, homelessness, illiteracy and environmental degradation.

And even the most impartial members of the Royal Family have lent their support to the cause. Some surprise was expressed when the Queen became personally involved, supporting the launch of unleaded petrol. The Royal Mews was filled with 10,000 balloons in February 1989 to start a campaign to encourage the conversion of vehicles to lead free fuel. And the Queen added further support by converting, where

Prince Charles with John Cleese as they appeared in a 'green' video.

possible, the vehicles in the Royal Household to run on lead-free petrol.

But for a family who have been brought up to respect the countryside it is no surprise. Prince Philip is said to have taught his children from an early age. "We tried to educate our children so that if they went on a picnic they should pick everything up. No one would ever know there had been a picnic here."

This message of preservation rather than destruction has been one which all members of the Royal Family have adopted wherever possible. Both Prince Charles and Princess Anne encourage the organic approach on the lands around their own houses. Prince Charles has his own bottle bank, has long

OXFORD

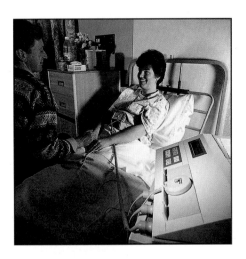 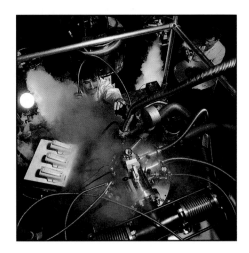

For over 30 years Oxford Instruments has pursued the application of scientific knowledge to the solution of problems in industry, healthcare and in centres of research and learning worldwide. This tradition of innovation is relevant and of value to society as a whole as well as to the international community of scientists and engineers and remains a cornerstone of policy for the company today and for the future.

We congratulate Her Majesty, Queen Elizabeth II, on the 40th Anniversary of her Accession, and wish her health and happiness in the years to come.

**Chairman and
Chief Executive Officer**

Deputy Chairman

since banned aerosols that are not ozone friendly and is discouraging the use of pesticides on his Highgrove estate.

On the Queen's Sandringham estate water meadows are left untouched, and 30 acres of reclaimed salt marsh have been agriculture on a large scale. Hedgerows have been replanted on the Royal estates. And at Balmoral in Scotland where, over 100 years ago, Queen Victoria began replanting forests which had been decimated to provide charcoal to fuel the industrial revolution, her

The estates surrounding Balmoral Castle, where forests have been carefully replanted and replaced since Queen Victoria's time.

converted into wet grassland with pools to attract waders and wild birds. At Highgrove, the home of the Prince and Princess of Wales, wild flower meadows and gardens can be found. Both Prince Philip and Prince Charles have been saddened by the disappearance of hedgerows from the British countryside and the resultant loss of wildlife, simply to make easier the mechanisation of descendants today vigorously continue the restoration, practising what they preach.

Long before another forty years have passed, it may be that the old phrase, "the wearing o' the green" will mean a happy tinge to the red, white and blue of the Union Jack. Indeed, can we not already salute the Royal family as Commanding Officers of the natural world's "Salvation Army?"

The Directors
of
THE RITZ CLUB
take pleasure in congratulating
Her Majesty Queen Elizabeth
on the occasion of
the 40th Anniversary
of Her accession
to the throne

A ROYAL PATRON

The Queen is patron of nearly 800 organisations which she supports as keenly as her time allows. Lt. Col. P.C.E. Creasy, OBE, FCIS, General Secretary of The Royal British Legion and Peter Elliott, Executive Administrator of the Entertainment Artists Benevolent Fund are two people whose associations enjoy the patronage of the Queen.

The Royal British Legion has been honoured by Royal patronage since its formation in 1921 when the then Prince of Wales agreed to become the Legion's first Patron. Her Majesty The Queen graciously agreed to continue the tradition on her accession to the throne in 1952 and has taken a close interest in the Legion and all matters made by Her Majesty in Council.

The Queen, who herself served in the ATS in World War II and many of the Royal Family, take an active part in the life of the Legion. This is nowhere better demonstrated than at the annual Royal British Legion Festival of Remembrance at the Royal Albert Hall, when without fail, there is the largest

The Queen reviews Scouts as she has done, as Patron of the Association, on a number of occasions.

relating to the welfare of the ex-service community over the intervening years.

The Legion is incorporated by Royal Charter which is in the gift of the Monarch. The Legion's original Charter was granted by King George V in 1925 and his successors have continued to grant supplemental Charters amending the original Charter. Amendments to the Royal Charter and Schedule of Rules may therefore only be

gathering of the Royal Family at any event outside of State ceremonies. The Queen Mother is President and a life member of the Legion's Women's Section, Prince Andrew has recently become President of the St James's Branch, the National Holding Branch of the Legion, while the Duke of Edinburgh, the Prince of Wales, the Duke of Kent and Prince Michael of Kent are all members of the Legion. In the week prior to

Remembrance Sunday Her Majesty receives Legion Poppy Sellers at Buckingham Palace.

Her Majesty has recently introduced the practise of a member of the Royal Family taking the salute of the ex-Services Contingent after the Cenotaph service. This parade consists of the ex-Service men, women and widows who attend the service in Whitehall and march afterwards to Horse Guards, where the salute is taken by the member of the Royal Family: a

Alexandra and Prince and Princess Michael of Kent.

The Queen was also present to celebrate the Legion's Golden Jubilee in 1971 when she honoured the Legion by conferring the prefix "The Royal" onto the British Legion. To mark the anniversary, the Queen named a RNLI lifeboat "The Royal British Legion" at a ceremony at Henley-on-Thames and held a special Garden Party for The Royal British Legion at Buckingham Palace in

The Queen visiting the Red Cross headquarters in Geneva, she is patron and president of the British Red Cross Association.

private parade, held without pomp or publicity.

Despite her heavy official programme, the Queen has been able to visit the Legion on many occasions: In 1962 she visited the Poppy Factory at Richmond, Surrey and she is to return there again in July 1992. The factory which started with five workers in the Old Kent Road in 1922, moved to Richmond in 1924 and today employs 115, mainly ex-Service and disabled workers. In the intervening years the Poppy Factory has been visited by the Queen Mother, the Princess Royal, the Duke and Duchess of York, Princess

August of that year.

In July 1977, the Queen's Silver Jubilee year, following a parade on Horse Guards reviewed by the Prince of Wales, the Queen and the Duke of Edinburgh reviewed the Legion's Standard Bearers on the East Lawn of Windsor Castle.

To mark the Legion's 60th Anniversary in 1981, the Queen attended a service held in Coventry Cathedral and in November officially opened the rebuilt Legion Headquarters at 48 Pall Mall.

The Queen grants the Legion' National President an annual audience at which she is briefed on the Legion's year. For example, in 1991 the President, General Sir Edward Burgess, was able to recount the highly successful 1990 Christmas parcels and amenities to Service men and women serving in the Gulf, how Christmas parties had been provided for their families left behind in Germany and also the help given to those serving in Northern Ireland. The President showed the Queen some of the many hundreds of letters of thanks received from individual Service personnel, Units and Commanders.

The Royal British Legion is extremely fortunate in having a patron who takes a keen interest in our benevolent work and encourages the other members of her family to do the same. The Legion's Officers and Members congratulate Her Majesty on her reign of forty years and while affirming their loyalty and affection, wish her very many more happy years as our Queen and Patron.

As patron of the Imperial Cancer Research Fund, the Queen visits research laboratories in London.

The Entertainment Artistes Benevolent Fund was founded in 1907, to take care of elderly performers who had fallen on hard times through no fault of their own. The funds to carry out this work depended on the income from small shows, donations and collections in the various music halls of the time.

In 1912 the EABF, or the Variety Artistes' Benevolent Fund as it was then, was honoured to have King George V command a Royal Variety Performance to take place in the presence of himself and the Queen. A second Command followed in

Children at The Royal Academy of Dancing enjoy a visit from their patron.

1919 as a mark of thanks for peace following World War I. King George wished to acknowledge the entertaining of troops which had taken place in France, Belgium and Europe, and requested that the Fund should receive the proceeds of this Command Performance.

From that date there has always been, except for a few rare occasions, a Royal the Fund. In November 1991 Princess Michael of Kent attended a dinner at the Banqueting House, Whitehall, which encompassed a performance by the young violinist Nigel Kennedy. The evening was a great success. Royal Variety Performances have been attended by the Queen Mother, Princess Margaret, Prince Charles, the Princess of Wales and the Duchess of York.

The Royal Variety Show has been an annual tradition for over 70 years.

Variety Performance, not a Command. The King became Patron of the Fund and this patronage has been handed from George V to George VI through to Queen Elizabeth II and Queen Elizabeth the Queen Mother.

The Royal Family support the Fund enthusiastically. It has been the custom in recent years for the Queen and the Queen Mother to rotate their attendance at the Royal Variety Performance. The Royal Family also attend other shows and functions for the EABF. In the last two years the Queen Mother has attended a Gala performance of Miss Saigon, in aid of the EABF, and also attended the opening of the Nursing Wing at Brinsworth House the residential home financed and supported by

For some 85 years a large number of the Fund's functions and shows have been graced by a member of the Royal Family, in particular the Queen or the Queen Mother. We are very aware of the generosity they extend to us in their busy lives and schedules. Without their patronage and continued support, the Fund would find it much more difficult to continue running Brinsworth House, or support the 250 beneficiaries who rely on the Fund's assistance.

We are extremely grateful to the Royal Family for their support over so many years and hope that this will continue to be a part of our cornerstone for many more years.

The Queen shares the role of patron of the Entertainment Artistes' Benevolent Fund with the Queen Mother. It is in aid of this fund that the Royal Variety Show is held each year.

A ROYAL PATRON

THE PALACE AND THE PRESS

How has the relationship between the monarch and the media changed over the last forty years? Douglas Keay, author of Elizabeth II, Portrait of a Monarch (Ebury), looks at the developments and influences over the decades.

On February 6 1952, as the young Queen Elizabeth prepared to fly home from Kenya, press photographers waiting at Nanyuki airport did an extraordinary thing. Instead of taking pictures, they rested their cameras on their arms, the lenses dipped towards the ground. Thus they showed respect for the late King, and thus they missed the chance of the very first pictures of the new monarch.

Today such behaviour would neither be expected, nor requested. In forty years the attitudes of the monarchy and the media, each to the other, has changed enough that the Queen would expect pictures to be taken and newspaper readers and television viewers would be more than surprised if they did not receive them.

"Above all this our royalty is to be reverenced," wrote Walter Bagehot, the constitutional expert in 1867. "In its mystery is its life. We must not let daylight in upon magic."

At the outset of her reign probably the majority of the Queen's subjects would have agreed with Bagehot. Indeed polls taken at the time show that two years after the coronation 34% of those questioned believed that the Queen had been specially chosen by God, and by 1964 the number had dropped only to 30%. Such was the respect shown to the monarch that the first task of a Fleet Street reporter appointed to the job of Court Correspondent was to buy himself a bowler hat, and, it was reported at the time, those standing in pubs watching the Queen's coronation on the nine inch television screens of those days felt it incumbent to remove their caps.

Respect had not always been shown to royalty. Eighteenth century kings were lampooned regularly and even Queen Victoria was popularly cartooned as "Mrs Brown". However, following the abdication of Edward VIII, which had threatened to destroy the monarchy, and the reign of the greatly loved King George VI, the young new Queen was welcomed as "a gleaming champion", to use Winston

The classic image of Royalty as seen in the early part of the Queen's reign.

The coronation in 1953 was the first major Royal event to be televised, heralding a new era for British royalty.

Churchill's description, who might herald a New Elizabethan Age in an austerity bludgeoned post-war world.

The Queen has never seen a need to hire a public relations firm either to burnish her own image — "I am not a film-star" or surreptitiously to promote the monarchy — there is no election for a sovereign. But she does have a Press Secretary, who in turn has a small staff — less than a dozen — to take care of the Queen's 400 public engagements each year and the scores of Press enquiries from around the world that pour into Buckingham Palace day and night.

Up until 1968 the Press Secretary was a former naval officer, Commander Richard Colville, whose certain belief was that "if there comes a time when the British monarchy ever needs a real public-relations officer, the institution of monarchy in this country will be in serious decline." He was liked and admired by his staff, but thought of

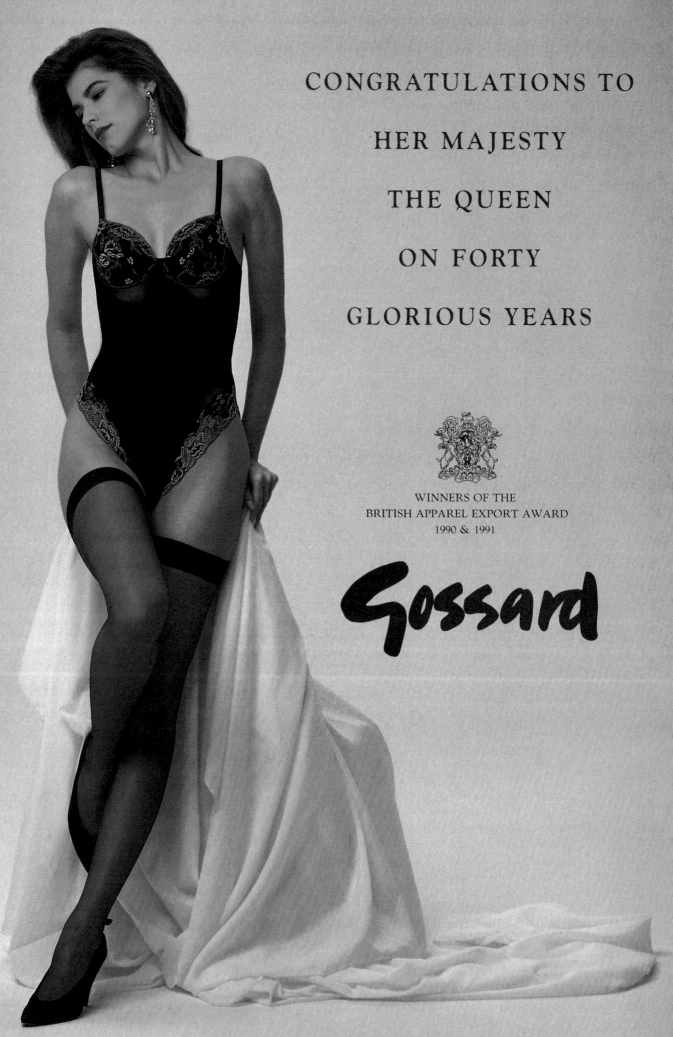

CONGRATULATIONS TO

HER MAJESTY

THE QUEEN

ON FORTY

GLORIOUS YEARS

WINNERS OF THE
BRITISH APPAREL EXPORT AWARD
1990 & 1991

Gossard

differently by Fleet Street — partly because of his brusque manner. Reporters accused him of treating them like tradesmen.

In the mid-nineteen sixties — the "swinging sixties" — the monarchy, in common with other long established institutions in Britain, began to come under harsh scrutiny. In an editorial in 1967 the

'A young Queen and a young family was infinitely newsworthy' according to Prince Philip.

Sunday Telegraph, not known for republican views, noted "a marked change in the public's attitude to the Crown." Many young people regarded the Queen as "an arch square". And, opined the editorial, the British monarchy might not be swept away in anger but "swallowed in a great and growing yawn."

The Queen was almost certainly aware of the feeling, but it is not in her nature to make dramatic or sudden changes. Prince Philip believed that the monarchy was still part of the fabric of the nation, but that the situation had altered since 1952. "A young Queen and a young family," he told a local television audience in 1968, "was infinitely more newsworthy and amusing. Now we're getting on for middle age, and I dare say when we're really ancient, there might be a bit more reverence again. For the present, people either can't stand us, or they think we're all right."

Commander Colville's successor as the

Queen's Press Secretary — he took over in 1968 — was an Australian with an invigorating outlook on life. Bill Heseltine, subsequently Sir William Heseltine, who became the Queen's Private Secretary and retired in 1990 after 27 years royal service, was chief amongst those responsible for pulling the royal family out of the doldrums of public regard, at a time when there was no Princess of Wales or Duchess of York to quicken interest.

Heseltine realised that the royal family were no longer "rounded" figures in the public imagination. "One had ceased to know anything about them, except what one read in the gossip columns or in the official announcements. Neither of these seemed a very satisfactory way of depicting the life of the royal family."

The answer, as it turned out, was to be a television documentary about the Queen called 'Royal Family'. Made with the participation of the Queen and her family, the film attracted an initial audience in July 1969 of 23 million and went on, with four repeats, to be seen by some 40 million viewers over a period of eighteen months.

Princess Anne's trip to Kenya for the television programme Blue Peter was another Royal first.

The film's fascination lay in letting in a little light on Bagehot's royal "magic" — though there were some who saw dangers. "Every institution that has so far attempted to use TV to popularise or aggrandise itself has been diminished and trivialised by it," wrote one critic. A famous anthropologist warned that "if any member of the tribe ever sees inside the chief's hut then the whole

Sir William Heseltine is credited with changing the image of the Royal family during his time as Press Secretary.

system of the tribal system is damaged and the tribe eventually disintegrates."

Notwithstanding these reservations, since 1969 the royal family — the Prince of Wales in particular — has increasingly used television as a main outlet for its ideas and depiction, with varying degrees of success. However it is worth noting that the Queen herself waited twenty-three years before agreeing to another film being made about her life and it will be interesting to see whether the latest documentary, *Elizabeth R* marking the 40th anniversary of the Queen's accession, enjoys the extended term of popularity of its predecessor — if only because all branches of the media over the years have ensured that there is less mystery surrounding the monarchy than there was in 1969. Some fear a diminution of the royal family's dignity by becoming as familiar as characters in a soap-opera.

Elizabeth II is the first British monarch of what has been called the Television Age. Her father, George VI, had refused to allow television cameras to record his daughter's wedding, but the Queen wished her subjects to have the chance of seeing her coronation — even though her Prime Minister Winston

Churchill growled "I don't see why the BBC should have a better view of my monarch being crowned than me." He later relented.

Television whets the public appetite to know even more about those parts of the royal family's life that television does not choose, or is not allowed, to reach. Paradoxically nowadays it also pokes merciless fun at the monarchy in some of its comedy programmes.

Throughout the 1970s newspapers and magazines — not normally complimented with the same kind of access to royalty as television — increasingly sought to satisfy the people's appetite and, thereby, increase sales.

In terms of number of column inches and pictures, coverage reached its zenith in the 1980s. The engagement and subsequent marriage of Lady Diana Spencer — "Lady Di" to the world — placed severe strains on the limited resources of Buckingham Palace Press Office but gave Fleet Street a welcome bonanza. What it could not confirm, it speculated upon.

Unfortunately for her, until she became officially engaged, Lady Diana did not qualify for Palace protection. And so, for weeks on end, her footsteps were dogged wherever she went. Her mother complained in a letter to The Times, and the Daily Mirror responded: "If Lady Diana Spencer is

Media coverage reached its zenith in the 1980s.

to be the future Queen of England she cannot expect to be Greta Garbo as well."

After the royal wedding in St Paul's Cathedral on July 29, 1981, watched by a world wide television audience estimated at over 700 million, the Queen and her advisers expected media attention to slacken, but it did not. The imagination and admiration of the world had been swept up in a whirl by the model-girl looks and fashion of the Princess of Wales and it seemed that people

The Queen and the Duke of Edinburgh pictured with their grandchildren, typical of the more informal portrayal of the Royal family today.

could not see or read too much of her.

At that stage, the Princess of Wales was not mentally ready to withstand the continuous onslaught of media attention — however much she appeared to be putting on a brave and smiling face. When it was learned that she was expecting her first child, public interest naturally increased, as did the pressure. So much so that the Queen felt obliged to step in, calling Fleet Street editors to Buckingham Palace to make her concern known, in the hope that they would desist from their constant attention for at least a decent interval. For the most part they sympathised, and duly obliged.

In the decade since Prince William was born, relations between Buckingham Palace and Fleet Street have remained good, guarded but on the whole calm. Each appreciates what the other's job is, but their aims can never be entirely the same. From time to time the marriage of the Prince and Princess of Wales has been examined for cracks, and the Duchess of York has apparently still to find full favour with the Press. The Princess of Wales continues to dance the light fantastic and over a space of almost eleven years has gained an ever increasing admiration for her dedication to good causes. But during **forty** years the Queen has not put a foot wrong.

We may never again see a time when, out of respect, Press photographers rest their cameras on their arms and dip their lenses to the ground. But that does not mean that the media as a whole is not as loyal as ever it was to the monarchy, or that it does not have a deep admiration and respect for the Queen personally.

For Her Majesty's part, as a senior member of the Household once pointed out to me, "The Queen can see as clearly as anybody that the institution which she represents and embodies depends quite heavily on the impact it makes through the media."

Development is a process by which people grow and learn to live significantly. The House of Angostura, in existence for over 150 years, now produces and ships its aromatic bitters to over 100 countries of the world from Trinidad and Tobago, a country greatly assisted in its development by membership in the Commonwealth of Nations.

Angostura has been granted the Royal Warrant of Appointment to successive generations of the British Monarchy and is honoured to join this 40th Anniversary Tribute to Her Majesty. We thank Her for the outstanding contribution She has made to the development of Nations and wish Her and the Royal Family continued health and happiness in the years ahead.

Thomas Gatcliffe

Chairman

THROUGH THE CAMERA LENS

Covering the Royal Family on tour can be difficult and exhausting particularly with heavy photographic equipment. Ronald G. Bell MVO, Press Association Court Photographer from 1976 to 1990 talks about the trials and tribulations as well as the pleasure and enjoyment of touring with the Queen.

The Queen's overseas engagements can broadly be divided into two categories, visits to a particular country usually for up to about a week, and tours visiting several countries, which sometimes extend over several weeks. The Jubilee Tour in 1977 of Australia, New Zealand, and the South Pacific Islands of Tonga, Fiji, Papua New Guinea and Samoa took nearly eight weeks, and her first tour of the same area in 1953 even longer. But these were exceptional and a period of two to three weeks is more usual.

The first official news of an overseas visit or tour by the Queen comes several months in advance, in a brief two or three line announcement in the list of Royal engagements. This merely gives the names of the countries and approximate dates of the visits. Later a fuller programme with a general outline of the itinerary is made available by Buckingham Palace, with the request that all photographers wishing to cover the tour apply for accreditation to the Press Office. Most of the applications will come from photographers who regularly cover the activities of the Royal Family and are therefore well known to the Press Office, but all are vetted.

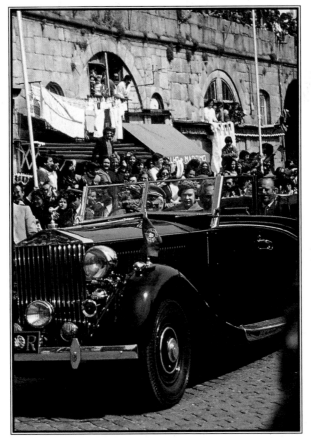

The Queen and Duke of Edinburgh paid an official State Visit to Portugal in 1985.

The arrangements for a Royal visit or tour abroad are made jointly by Buckingham Palace, the Foreign Office through the local Embassy or High Commission, and the appropriate government department of the host countries. All approved applications are passed to them so that they will have some idea of the amount of media interest from the UK.

Several weeks beforehand a party from Buckingham Palace, consisting of among others the Queen's Private Secretary, Her Personal Police Officers and Press Secretary, make a recce to finalise the arrangements. The Press Secretary negotiates with the local officials to establish the best camera positions not only for accessibility, but also for light. There is no point, for example, in having the camera position for an airport arrival looking straight into the sun. He also sorts out travel arrangements and hotel accommodation. This is fairly straightforward if it is a visit to one country,

Congratulations
to Her Majesty Queen Elizabeth II

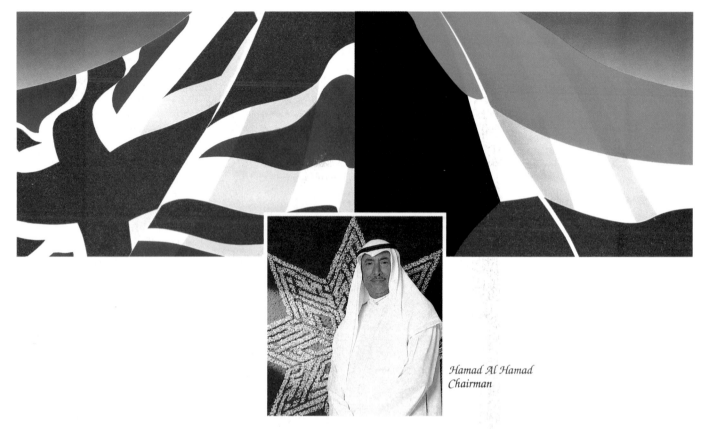

Hamad Al Hamad
Chairman

*We congratulate Her Majesty on the 40th Anniversary of Her Accession.
Remembering the long-standing friendship between our two peoples,
we extend our gratitude for the outstanding contribution
of her armed forces to the recent liberation of our country.*

*We also thank Her Majesty for her concern for the
degradation caused by the wanton burning of our oilfields.
We also salute Her Majesty and her family for their dedication to
environmental protection, a matter of vital importance to our world's future.*

البنك التجاري الكويتي
Commercial Bank of Kuwait

P.O. Box 2861 Safat, 13029 – Safat – Kuwait. Telex 22004 – Telefax 2450150 – Telephone 2411001.

because the Press will probably all stay in the one hotel, returning each evening at the end of the day's engagements. The problem becomes much more complicated when on tour, and the Press have to be transported not only from town to town but also country to country, always endeavouring to be one step ahead of the Royals.

because many of the visits overlap and also in these days of budgets there is the question of cost. So the photographer has to be selective. The decision whether to cover a particular visit or tour can be a difficult one. Although the photographer has made an initial application for accreditation and had it approved, it is not necessarily binding, but

The Government House gardens, Port of Spain, part of the Queen's 1985 Caribbean tour when she visited Trinidad and Tabago.

On their return, a final itinerary for the tour is circulated to all who have approved accreditation, with detailed arrangements for photo coverage, internal travel arrangements and accommodation, and most important approximate costs. Although there have been exceptions, usually the Press are responsible for getting themselves to the start of the tour and back home at the end. But internal travel while covering the tour and also hotel accommodation is arranged by the host country with the photographers settling their own bills.

During any one year a great many overseas engagements are carried out by the Royal Family, and the photographers who specialise in covering the Royals would like to cover all of them. This is not possible, however,

when all the additional information becomes available a decision has to be made to proceed or not. The different photographers and the organisations they work for all have varying criteria in making their decision but basically take into account whether the visit or tour has a great news or political significance? How good are the photo opportunities? What are the difficulties in getting material back to the office — processing and transmitting film? How long is the tour and does it clash with any other important Royal occasions — home or abroad? Will the pictures have any great value for Library purposes? The cost — with a news organisation this will have to be doubled as a reporter will probably go as well.

If the decision is to go ahead, then the

Our very best wishes on the occasion of this fortieth anniversary celebration.

You are a champion of people around the world bringing happiness, respect and love to all. Indeed, you are the Lady of the Century.

You brought great joy to Miami, Florida during your visit last year and left lasting memories with both the city and its people.

In HRH, Prince Charles, you have given us a great leader, philanthropist and dedicated world public servant. Following your example, he has been a great inspiration to us all whether in the protection of our environment, promoting superb architecture or in leading the great movement of the United World Colleges around the world. We who know him share in your pride.

May God bless you and give you good health to continue your great work for many years to come.

With admiration and respect,

Louise H. Courtelis

Alec P. Courtelis

Alec and Louise Courtelis

photographer will confirm his application and send his passport and any other personal details required through to the countries involved. There will be a general press pass for the whole tour, but each individual country will also want to issue its own. Checks must be made for any necessary visas and also inoculations, although most press photo-travel well; also they needed a print. This meant not only did the photographer have to go on the tour armed with a list of possible places to have his film developed and printed at the stopover points, but also the locations of the nearest transmitter which could well be miles away in a main telephone exchange or newspaper office.

The Queen became the first British monarch to address Congress during her 1991 State Visit to the USA.

graphers keep the latter up to date as a matter of routine. All these preliminaries over, they aim to arrive at the tour's starting point a couple of days before the Queen. Here they have a full briefing on the final programme.

When working overseas the biggest headache is not always taking the pictures, but getting them back to the office. The methods used have changed dramatically over the last few years. On earlier Royal Tours all the material taken would be air freighted back to London each day, including TV films. The photographers working for magazines and using transparencies still employ this method. It entails many hours on the telephone before leaving, checking flight times, arranging couriers, and also if needed (and it usually is) persuading airport cargo officers to accept parcels out of office hours.

Newspaper and agency photographers now use transmitters to send their pictures over telephone lines back to London. Picture transmitters have been around a long time, but they were heavy and did not

Each print took about 15-20 minutes to send, and if there were a number of photographers with several prints each, it was a lengthy process. There was always a race to be first in the queue. All this after a long day covering the tour.

Most photographers have stories to tell of the trials and tribulations of processing and transmitting. One I remember well happened in 1982 on a tiny Pacific island. There were just two Fleet Street photographers, a Daily Express man and myself, and we had discovered, much to our surprise, that there was a transmitter on the island. The Police Chief offered us the use of his darkroom in the police station, for which we were very thankful. We were less enthusiastic on arriving at the station, however, when several small piglets were chased out. The temperature was in the nineties and the atmosphere inside was rather high. On the shelves were numerous bottles, all without labels containing rather dubious liquids, and a very dilapidated

What mankind can dream, technology can achieve...

The most advanced microchip plant in the world, Fujitsu Microelectronics Limited, County Durham, was officially opened by Her Majesty the

Queen only months before the 40th anniversary of the accession.

In an era of constant change, Fujitsu has led the world in information technology, telecommunications and semiconductor manufacture.

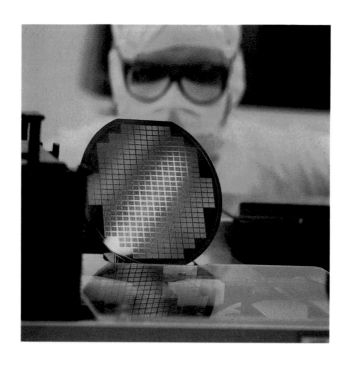

enlarger. We identified what we thought was developer and decided to risk developing one film each. Amazingly they turned out quite well and we were able to produce a couple of reasonable prints. These we delivered to the telephone exchange with the request that they should be wired to the appropriate London numbers. As

pictures are sent direct from the negative, and a print is produced at the receiving end. These machines are quite small, about the size of a large typewriter, and although still quite heavy, are easily transportable. They can transmit in either black and white or colour. Now photographers process their films in hotel bathrooms and plug their

Nothing is left out of the organisation of Royal tours — name tags mark the spot when the Queen and President Bush meet players after a baseball match.

there was a delay we decided to leave the prints, have a meal and return later, which we did. The operator assured me that my prints had gone but a sixth sense prompted me to check. Indeed they had gone — to Hong Kong! Luckily there was still time to send them to London.

The introduction of negative transmitters has changed all this. As the name suggests

transmitting machines into the telephone. It means an even longer working day and a chaotic bedroom but at least one has the benefit of room service.

Although this machine has simplified the transmitting process, it has added considerably to the weight of equipment which each photographer has to transport around. With several bags of camera and

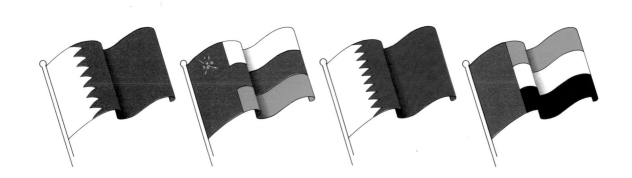

THE STATE OF BAHRAIN,
THE SULTANATE OF OMAN,
THE STATE OF QATAR,
AND THE UNITED ARAB EMIRATES
SALUTE
HER MAJESTY QUEEN ELIZABETH II
- GULFAIRSTYLE.

Gulf Air proudly carries the flags of four Gulf States to four continents, serving over three million passengers a year - a far cry from 1950, when a young British aviator planned to operate an air taxi between four Gulf cities.

After 20 years growing within the region, Gulf Air spread the wings of our Golden Falcon Service internationally to become the fully-fledged national carrier of the four owner-states.

Manifesting the great affection our people bear Her Majesty Queen Elizabeth II, the Golden Falcon is honoured to carry the salute of our owner-States to the 40th Anniversary of the Accession.

GULF AIR FLIES FROM LONDON DIRECT TO THE GULF 22 TIMES WEEKLY.

The timeless splendour of Petra forms a magnificent backdrop for photographers capturing the two Royal couples during a State Visit to Jordan.

darkroom equipment plus personal luggage, the excess baggage charge can be rather high. The cameras used on tour are almost exclusively 35mm. Personally I always took four bodies plus a spare, and lenses ranging from 24mm through to 600mm. Zoom lenses are very popular, with the 80-200mm and 35-70mm being the most widely used.

The reason for so many camera bodies is that very often there is not time to change lenses, and the photographer needs a camera with the appropriate lens ready at all times.

Carrying this on one's shoulder all day can be very tiring and many photographers experience back trouble. Tripods are never carried, a monopod being preferred.

One other essential item of equipment is a small aluminium step ladder. Very handy for getting viewpoints over the heads of the

even of the tour. After travelling half way round the world this does not go down well with Editors back home, who tend not to appreciate the situation.

The Walkabout has become a feature of most of the Queen's tours. It could be an impromptu one of just a few yards before

With Sheik Abdullah Jabir the Queen watches a dancing display in Kuwait during a Middle East Tour in 1979.

crowds or the other pressmen if you arrive late on the scene. If space is limited, for example on a narrow pavement, three rows of cameramen can be accommodated with the aid of ladders; front row kneeling, middle standing and the rear on ladders — very useful.

When covering a day's engagements with the Queen the photographers are often transported at the rear of the motorcade, leaping out at each stop. If this is not possible because of security problems or the numbers involved, the Press group is divided into two, with each group covering alternate engagements. This arrangement is not popular because it often happens that one or other misses the best picture of the day, or

getting into her car, or a planned one of several hundred yards along a main street. Although popular with the Royals and the public, they provide a headache for the security officers and the photographers. The latter try to maintain a distance of about 7 to 10 yards, backing away in front of the Queen and stopping when she does. With today's modern lenses they do not need to be any closer and do not obstruct the view of the public, provided the area between themselves and the Queen is kept clear. Although not taking shots all the time it is important to be there, just in case any incidents occur — pleasant or otherwise. This is one of the main differences between reporters and photographers. While the reporters would obviously prefer to see first hand any incident that happens, if they miss it they can write a report from accounts of other eye witnesses. Not so the photographers. They have to be on the spot all the time. Blink once, stop to change a lens,

them, and there would not be enough room for all of us in that spot, what started off as walking pace soon developed into a full scale charge. Those who arrived first stopped as instructed, but the late arrivals thundered into the back of them. It all ended in a great undignified melée at the Queen's feet. She

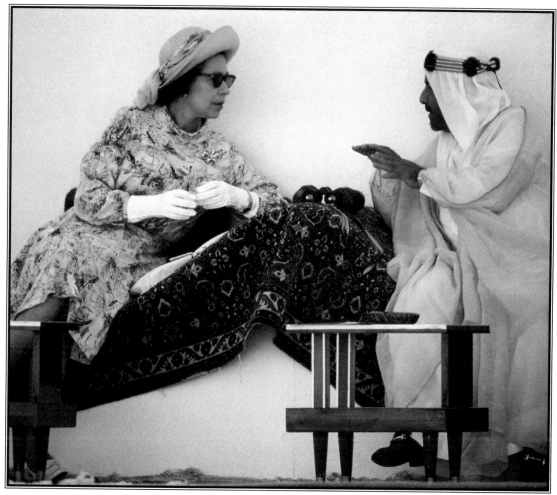

At the racecourse with the Amir of Bahrain, the Queen probably discussing one of her favourite subjects — horses.

and the picture could be missed.

A great deal of planning goes into the Press arrangements but sometimes things do go wrong. During the tour of the Gulf States in 1979 the Queen was entertained by King Khalid of Saudi Arabia to a night banquet in the desert. It was pitch black when we arrived and the King and Queen were already seated in a long open-sided tent some fifty yards away. This was a good photo opportunity, and as well as the photographers on the tour there were also many local photographers. We were asked to proceed in an orderly fashion and stop a few yards from the Royals. But as the best picture was going to be immediately in front of

was not amused — and of course it spoilt all the pictures. The lesson learned that night was that in similar situations photographers should be pre-positioned.

Normally the Queen is very co-operative and well aware of the photographers' needs. If approached through her Press Secretary for a special picture, she will usually agree, provided that it does not interfere or cause any disruption in the day's events. One such occasion was in 1983. The Queen and the Duke of Edinburgh were in Kenya visiting Tree Tops, where she had been staying in 1952 when she heard the news of the death of her father, King George V1. The shot we all wanted was the Queen with Tree Tops in the background. We had all hired cars and driven for some hours to get there, but it obviously was not going to work without being posed. We made our request, knowing that if she said "Yes" she would have a long walk around the waterhole in front of Tree Tops to reach the ideal spot. She did agree, and for good measure brought with her the

odd day to relax. There are very few days off. One seems to be constantly packing and unpacking photo and personal equipment. Very often there is an early morning start and sometimes one arrives back at the hotel in the evening with just enough time to do a quick change into a dinner jacket and rush off to cover an evening engagement. And

A perfect picture for the photographers during the 1975 State Visit to Japan.

Chief Hunter complete with safari suit and rifle — a little touch which added a great deal to the picture.

During a tour the Queen will host many receptions, but she always finds time to hold at least one for the media. These are popular occasions when one can chat informally to her, and particularly so if held on board The Britannia where they serve rather large gin and tonics.

It is only when the Queen is using the Royal Yacht to sail from one point to another that the media, who fly ahead of her, get the

always an hour has to be found to send pictures back to the office, either during the day or last thing at night, depending on the time difference. Even getting laundry done can become a major headache.

So altogether tours are a somewhat exhausting business, and although one travels to some of the most interesting and exotic places in the world, the schedule is so tight, that one seldom has the chance to really see and appreciate them. Nevertheless, covering a Royal Tour is a unique and memorable experience.

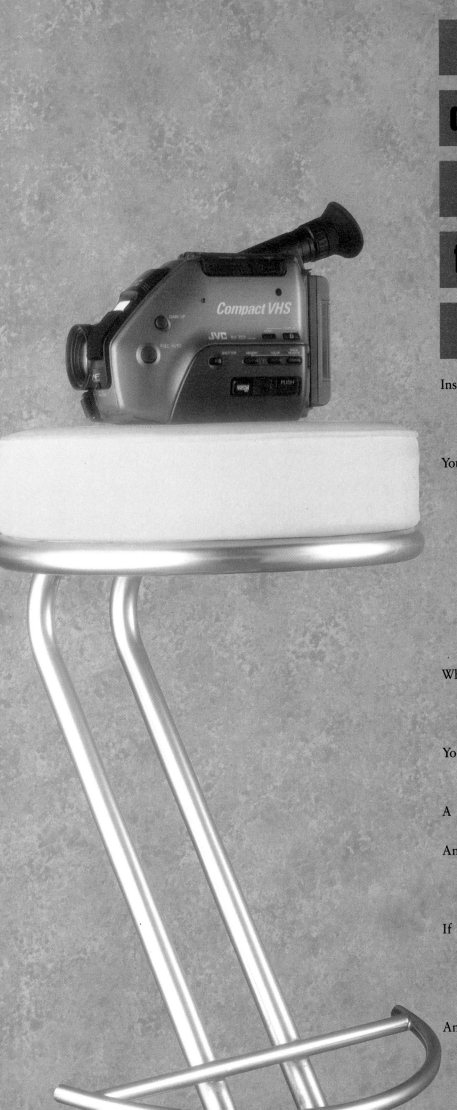

Why risk a blind date, when JVC have the perfect match for your VHS?

Instant attraction. Love at first sight. Whatever you like to call it, that's what always happens when a VHS machine is introduced to the JVC GR-AX10 camcorder.

You see, the GR-AX10 is designed for total compatibility with all VHS machines. (Not so surprising, when you consider JVC invented the VHS format.)

What else makes the GR-AX10 such a catch? Well, you don't have to mess around with leads like you do with certain other camcorders.

You get the benefit of an 8 times power zoom. Low-light capability for those intimate moments.

A snap-on DC video lamp for when the lights are out.

And the fact that our camcorder uses compact tapes makes them very easy to send to friends and relatives here and abroad.

If you've got a wedding, christening, day out, party or holiday coming up – or a toddler growing up – see your JVC dealer.

JVC
USE OUR IMAGINATION.

And make a date with the GR-AX10. Then you can look forward to many happy years together.

Maples would like
to offer their
Congratulations
to Her Majesty the Queen
on the 40th anniversary
of her accession
to the throne.

We're celebrating our own anniversary this year
150 years of fine furnishings and carpets

HOMES AND PALACES

Dr John Martin Robinson, MA, D.Phil, F.S.A., Maltravers Herald of Arms, Librarian to the Duke of Norfolk and an independent historic buildings consultant, looks at the Royal residences of Britain, the homes and the palaces, their history and their architecture.

The royal residences as they exist today are the product of several centuries of evolution. They fall into two basic categories: palaces intended for the occupation of the monarch as Head of State, and private houses intended as retreats from official life. The latter are not very different from other large country houses, but the former have a as private residences by other members of the Royal Family, such as Kensington Palace and Clarence House, or ones that are no longer occupied at all but are preserved as museums open to the public, of which Hampton Court and Osborne on the Isle of Wight are notable examples.

The extant royal residences are of very

The Throne Room at Buckingham Palace contains a number of thrones, including the Chairs of Estate, used during the first part of the Queen's Coronation.

more ceremonial and formal character with guards of honour and state rooms for official functions as well as private accommodation for the Royal Family and Household.

Sandringham and Balmoral are the principal private houses of the Queen, while Buckingham Palace and Windsor Castle, and to a lesser extent St. James's and Holyroodhouse, are Her Majesty's official residences. There are also a number of subsidiary houses and palaces which are used varied origins. Windsor Castle has been a royal home since the time of William the Conqueror. St. James's occupies the site of a medieval leper hospital acquired and rebuilt by Henry VIII as a hunting lodge. Holyroodhouse, the Scottish royal palace, developed out of the guest house of Holyrood Abbey in the fifteenth century and was rebuilt by Charles II. Buckingham Palace was bought by George III for his wife Queen Charlotte, and reconstructed by George IV. Balmoral was acquired as a holiday home by Queen Victoria in 1848 and the present house built by her and Prince Albert in 1853. The Sandringham estate was purchased for Edward VII as Prince of Wales in 1863 and he erected the present house in 1869-70.

The royal residences of Britain have an interest beyond their basic architectural the Palace of Westminster fulfilled that role. Henry VIII took over Whitehall Palace from Cardinal Wolsey and Whitehall was occupied by succeeding Tudor and Stuart monarchs till it burnt down in 1698. In the eighteenth century St. James's became the metropolitan royal palace and seat of the court, which is why foreign diplomats in

The Centre Room at Buckingham Palace. The Palace has been the official London residence of the Sovereign since the mid-nineteenth century.

quality. They represent the longest continuous tradition in Europe (apart from the Papacy) and form the setting for the oldest and grandest surviving monarchy. Their story reflects the development and vicissitudes of that monarchy over a period of a thousand years. The royal residences have developed with the institution of monarchy and reflect its history in their architecture. Though the general pattern of the royal palaces and houses has not changed in this century, the present reign has seen several new developments and architectural improvements.

Buckingham Palace, now the principal royal palace in London, is perhaps the best known of the royal residences but it was not originally built as such. In the Middle Ages

London are still accredited to the Court of St. James. The private apartments at St. James's were in turn destroyed by fire in 1806, and on succeeding to the throne in 1820 George IV took over his mother's house and reconstructed and enlarged it to the design of John Nash. The original house had been built by John Sheffield, Duke of Buckingham, in the late seventeenth century. It only ceased to be private property when acquired by George III following his marriage to Charlotte of Mecklenburg-Strelitz in 1761. The dignified front with the famous balcony overlooking the Mall was added by Queen Victoria and re-faced with Portland stone in 1910 to the design of Aston Webb.

The Grand Staircase at Windsor Castle made for Queen Victoria in 1866 by the architect Anthony Salvin.

*Congratulations to Her Majesty the Queen
on the 40th anniversary of her reign.*

Royal Doulton

THE WORLD'S LEADING FINE CHINA COMPANY

ROYAL CROWN DERBY · MINTON · ROYAL ALBERT · ROYAL DOULTON

ROYAL DOULTON LIMITED MINTON HOUSE LONDON ROAD STOKE-ON-TRENT STAFFORDSHIRE ST4 7QD

George IV's palace, built of Bath stone, still survives behind and forms the largest part of the present structure. It has a handsome facade with a domed bow overlooking the private garden, and a two-tier portico in the Quadrangle which forms the Grand Entrance for use on state occasions. Nash's architecture is a Frenchy

their own private entrance from the side.

They include the Luncheon Room, an exotic Chinese interior created with fittings and furniture originally made for Brighton Pavilion and brought here when Queen Victoria sold the Prince Regent's 'pleasure dome' to Brighton Corporation. Many of these rooms have been refurbished in the

The Queen's Presence Chamber at Windsor Castle, one of three rooms at the castle originally made by Charles II, for his Queen, Catherine.

neo-classicism expressive of George IV's personal taste. George IV formed the best collection of French furniture ever assembled and most of this survives and adorns the principal rooms of Buckingham Palace today. The State Rooms are on the first floor and are elaborately detailed with rich gilded plaster ceilings and carved marble chimneypieces by the leading early nineteenth century English sculptors. The Blue, White and Green Drawing Rooms, the Music Room and Throne Room are among the most original and opulent rooms of their type. Together with the huge ballroom added by Queen Victoria, they form a splendid setting for investitures, diplomatic receptions and the state visits of foreign heads of state.

The private rooms of the Queen are on the north side of the quadrangle and have

present reign, including the Queen's Audience Chamber. This was decorated by John Fowler, the leading post-war English interior-designer, with turquoise blue and white walls and hand-painted satin cushions with crowns and other royal emblems. Another major innovation by the Queen and Prince Philip was the conversion in the 1960s of the bomb-damaged former chapel at the south west corner of the palace into the Queen's Gallery where popular changing exhibitions from the royal collections are shown to the public. It has a modern interior designed by Sir Hugh Casson, the former president of the Royal Academy and an architect who has given much advice to the Queen on alterations and restoration work at Buckingham Palace, Windsor Castle and Sandringham. Another designer who has

In full support
of the
Royal Anniversary Trust

had an important influence on new work at the palace is David Hicks, the interior decorator who is connected with the Royal Family through his marriage to Pamela, the younger daughter of Lord Mountbatten. David Hicks has designed some smart modern bathrooms and lavatories for guests.

Much of the ground floor, mezzanine and

as the presentation of the Queen's gift of gold on the Feast of the Epiphany. The proclamation of new monarchs also takes place at St. James's Palace with Garter King of Arms reading from a parchment scroll on the balcony in Friary Court.

Buckingham Palace is regarded by the Queen as her 'office' whereas Windsor Castle

The quadrangle at Windsor Castle with a statue of King Charles II in the foreground.

the south wing of the palace is occupied as offices by the Lord Chamberlain's Department and the Royal Household, the overflow of which is housed at St. James's Palace where the Chapel Royal is also situated, services being held alternately in the old Tudor Chapel and the beautiful Queen's Chapel designed by Inigo Jones for Henrietta Maria, wife of Charles I. St. James's is still the scene of many picturesque religious ceremonies such

is her home. Apart from being the largest, grandest and most historic of the royal palaces, Windsor has a special place in Her Majesty's affections because it was the house in which she was brought up, the Royal Family having spent most of the war there. As a result Windsor Castle rather than Sandringham has become the principal country house of the Royal Family in this reign, in contrast to Edward VII's and George

HATS OFF TO YOU, YOUR MAJESTY.

The Wimpey Group
congratulates H.M. The Queen
on forty glorious years.

V's preference for Sandringham. The Queen spends most of her weekends and Christmas at Windsor, as well as the traditional periods of residence of the court in April and during Ascot Week in June. Many state visits of foreign heads of state also take place now at Windsor. The Queen has also maintained the splendid ceremonial for the Garter

range adjoining the George IV Gateway. The Norman and medieval castle was transformed into a Baroque palace by Charles II and given its fairy tale Gothic appearance by George IV who employed Sir Jeffry Wyatville to remodel it in the 1820s. As well as creating the present dramatic silhouette with heightened towers and turrets, Wyatville was

The grounds around Lock Muick, part of the Balmoral Estates, have been designated as a wildlife reserve area since 1974.

Service, revived by her father King George VI. A series of impressive private family dances have taken place in the state rooms during the present reign, as well as traditional events like the Waterloo Banquet held each year in the Waterloo Chamber to celebrate the defeat of Napoleon.

Covering nearly twelve acres, Windsor is more like a little town than a house, and hundreds of people live within its confines including the dean and chapter of St. George's Chapel, the Military Knights of Windsor and many members of the Royal Household. The state rooms occupy the north block of the Upper Ward, with the Queen's private apartments in the south

responsible for much of the present interior. He transformed a warren into a well-planned house, notably by adding the Grand Corridor which runs for 500 feet round two sides of the quadrangle. As a result the castle has become very comfortable.

When staying at Chatsworth, which was also improved in the same way by Wyatville, the Queen said to the Duchess of Devonshire: 'So cosy. Just like Windsor'.

The present reign has seen many improvements at the castle. Over the last two or three years the whole place has been rewired and the foundations of the Norman Round Tower underpinned. Many of the rooms have been redecorated. The appropriately sombre re-colouring of the Waterloo Chamber, undertaken with the advice of Sir Hugh Casson, has enhanced the nineteenth century architectural character of the room. Sir Hugh has also designed a series of new guest suites. Many of the state rooms have been re-hung with specially woven damask, and the pictures and furniture re-arranged to

which is the second largest in Norfolk, after Holkham. In purely architectural terms Sandringham is not very distinguished. It is a large, comfortable, hospitable and solid house. It was designed by A. J. Humbert, an architect much employed by the Victorian royal family 'for no very good reason'. Substantial additions including a ballroom and bowling

Balmoral Castle, where the Queen and her family spend their summer break each year.

show them to better advantage. Some of the impressive aura of Windsor, especially when the castle is en fête, is due to the late Lord Plunkett, Deputy Master of the Household and a personal friend of the Queen's. He had a considerable knowledge of furniture and pictures and very good taste; he was responsible for such inspired ideas as the decoration of the rooms on special occasions with fully-grown mock-orange bushes in pots.

Though Windsor has taken over some of the place of Sandringham, the Queen still spends the early part of the year at her great-grandfather's Norfolk house, and she and Prince Philip have undertaken many improvements on the 20,000 acre estate

alley were made to the east in 1892 by Colonel R. W. Edis. At the time when appreciation of Victorian architecture was at a low ebb in the late 1950s and 1960s it was even considered demolishing and rebuilding Sandringham. A design for a new house in 'the style of our time' was commissioned from David Roberts, the Modernist Cambridge architect. The Queen thought this scheme was too drastic and instead the existing house was rationalised and modernised under the direction of Hugh Casson who curtailed the service areas and devised new bedroom suites. With its sporting pictures, big game trophies, evocative Edwardian mementoes and royal portraits, the house now seems an attractive period-piece, and in recent years the Queen has opened it to the public in the summer.

The official royal palace in Scotland is Holyroodhouse in Edinburgh. Although rebuilt by Charles II in 1671-1678, this was a political gesture, and apart from Bonnie Prince Charlie in 1745 no member of the royal family occupied the present building but like a country gentleman's house.' As a result many of the rooms are relatively small and comfortable. The only large room is the ballroom, sixty-eight feet long, intended for the Ghillies' Dances which are still a great feature of the Balmoral scene. The castle retains much of its original furniture (made by Holland's of London) and decoration. The

Sandringham House sits in an area of 'Outstanding Natural Beauty' on the Norfolk coast. Used by the Royal Family for two months each year, the house was opened to the public for the first time in 1977.

before the twentieth century. George V and Queen Mary began the restoration of the palace and this has continued into the present reign. The Queen is usually in residence for a short time in June each year when she presides over various official functions including the Scottish garden parties. Her real home in Scotland is Balmoral in Aberdeenshire, where she spends several months in the late summer.

Balmoral was created entirely by Queen Victoria and Prince Albert. It was designed for them by William Smith, the son of an Aberdeen architect nicknamed 'Tudor Johnnie', and Prince Albert instructed him that the building should be 'not like a palace, latter is surprisingly bright and cheerful, making much use of tartan for wallpaper, chintzes and carpets, supplemented by a plentiful supply of antlers and Scotch thistles. Lord Clarendon commented that the chintzes would 'rejoice the heart of a donkey.' A member of the royal family remarked that the rooms were 'more patriotic than artistic.' The house is none the worse for that. Much of the fabric survives as left by Queen Victoria, and life at Balmoral is still much the same as in her time with fishing and stalking and picnics in the hills. The only major change is that, whereas Queen Victoria had only one village policeman outside, now there is a more formal guard of uniformed sentries.

A great heritage.

LLOYD'S

LLOYD'S OF LONDON

Lloyd's of London congratulates Her Majesty The Queen on the
fortieth anniversary of Her accession.

LLOYD'S
LLOYD'S OF LONDON

The name that covers the Earth.

THE ROYAL PURSE

The question of Royal finance, wealth and income are subjects for endless discussion and conjecture. Godfrey Talbot looks at the facts and how exactly the Royal Purse is divided up.

What does the throne cost? A question not easy to answer because, for one thing, relatively few figures are set out for scrutiny. And even earnest media discussion about these are often overlaid with wild arithmetic and wondrous guesswork. Newspaper readers are reminded that the Queen herself is a wealthy person

To be fair to gossip-column snipers who lack ammunition, even the main distributions of income and expenditure, let alone the minutiae, are so complex and partially disclosed that only some general quantifications are possible. But some facts may usefully be disclosed:

About 85 per cent of all expenditure

The Queen visiting Tutbury Castle, one of the Duchy of Lancaster castles.

(the estimates freely exaggerated) and yet does not pay income-tax, unlike everyone else in her family. Rarely is the point made that the Sovereign has this special tax-exemption by long-standing Parliamentary decree, and that nowadays the immunity is absolutely right in that Her Majesty directs large sums of 'royal income' straight into the national revenue in other ways — generous ways but as incalcuable as the duties and the taxes which the Queen *does* pay.

arising from the official duties of the Queen and others of the immediate Royal Family is met by Government departments. This expenditure includes, for example, the Royal Yacht *Britannia*, aircraft of the Queen's Flight, railway journeys in the United Kingdom, and the upkeep of what the accountants call 'the occupied palaces' (*not* the personally owned homes, Sandringham and Balmoral), of which the best known are

Buckingham Palace, Windsor Castle, St. James's Palace and Holyroodhouse in Edinburgh. In other words, these are great houses which belong to the State. Like the crown jewels and the royal collections of valuable pictures, the palaces are not personal property, but national heirlooms, not for disposal.

Sovereign but such items as the pay of judges and ambassadors. A revolutionary change came in the reign of George III — and it is the basis of modern practice. This change was to a system restricting the Civil List grants almost entirely to the monarch and close relatives (no non-royal officials).

The radical alteration was, and is, the

The Crown Jewels, like the various Royal Collections, are national heirlooms and not the personal property of the Queen.

One of the few sources of finance which are made public annually is the important and interesting one called The Civil List. The curious old name of this provision stems from a yearly gift of revenues granted by the House of Commons nearly three centuries ago to Stuart Sovereigns and then to their Georgian successors; but in those days it covered not only the maintenance of the

surrender to the State of the vast sums coming from the Sovereign's main hereditary revenues (the Crown Estate) in exchange for the very-much-smaller allowances paid by the State to the Royal House, the Civil List money.

So, today, there still exists — much publicised because there is little else to bite on — the Civil List annuity voted by

Parliament to the Queen from public funds. It is not in any sense a salary; it is an expense-allowance for the machinery of monarchy. And the annual sum now fixed by law for the Queen herself is £7,900,000. Parliament has stated that figure as the yearly sum for a decade, in estimation of need and inflation — but subject never-

refunded to the Treasury by the Queen — who also regularly gives a variety of financial help to certain other of her relatives, as well as to some 'servants of the Crown' who have retired after long service and may be in need.

An inspection of the Civil List's names manifests one remarkable omission: the Heir

The Veneto Vilio in Regents Park, part of the Crown Estate, the income from which the Queen surrenders to the Treasury.

theless to annual review; and the royal expenses are *strictly accountable*.

As part of the List, the Queen Mother, the Duke of Edinburgh, and certain other members of the immediate Royal Family receive smaller sums (roughly £2,000,000 between them). The allocations to the Duke of Gloucester, the Duke of Kent, Princess Alexandra of Kent and their Households are

to the Throne receives no money at all. The reason why there is not an allocation for the Prince of Wales is that he derives his income from the abundant revenues of the Duchy of Cornwall. As the sovereign's eldest son, he has been Duke of Cornwall ever since his mother's accession, when he was only three years old. Through the years, especially until he was 18, large sums of money from this

rich inheritance have flowed straight to the national exchequer; and, even at present, His Royal Highness voluntarily gives a quarter of all the revenues of the estates to the British Treasury.

The Cornwall duchy, incidentally, is not only the oldest but one of the largest of the royal properties in the country. Expertly

The income from the Crown Estate for the latest year declared was well over £60,000,000.

Sixty million yielded to the Chancellor of the Exchequer in return for that eight million or less voted to the Queen in the Civil List! It would seem to be an understatement to pronounce the 'swap' a good

Fish farming in Scotland one of the many varied sources of revenue from the Crown Estate.

managed and highly up-to-date in its practices, this princely inheritance owns some 130,000 acres of land in England and Wales (only about 20 per cent of it in Cornwall) and the holdings are spread across ten counties. The estates are for the most part farmland, but the Duchy also has commercial and residential property in the heart of London — including the Oval cricket ground!

To return to the Civil List and that 'revolution' in financing which began two centuries ago, the important point is that the List's expenses-money which goes to the Queen is relatively small compared with the sums she surrenders to the Treasury every year: the surplus revenues of the royal lands and properties which are hers by heredity: the Crown Estate (250,000 acres of agricultural land, but also — and far richer — big properties in central London and at Windsor, and more than half the United Kingdom's seashores).

bargain for the nation.

That may seem a layman's oversimplification of the accounts. But there is another good point. To judge even by everyday commercial yardsticks the upkeep of Britain's age-old ceremonials and their pageantry, and the maintenance costs of the *publicly visitable* great-houses (Windsor Castle and Sandringham, for instance) is well worthwhile, in any case, because the rituals and the residences are examples of the international attractiveness and plain profitability of British royalty. For the pageants and the palaces are a boon to the tourist industry, blessings to be counted in millions of pounds.

Besides the Civil List and a grant-in-aid, the other main source of income is The Privy Purse. This meets semi-official expenditure by the Queen as Sovereign; and the particular interest in the Purse money is that it comes from the net income of

Willis Faber & Dumas Limited,
54 Leadenhall Street,
London EC3.

Willis Corroon Group plc

Ten Trinity Square

London EC3P 3AX

The directors and staff worldwide of Willis Corroon
are proud to celebrate the 40th Anniversary of
Her Majesty The Queen's Accession to the Throne.

WILLIS CORROON
Insurance broker to the world

another distinct royal inheritance, the Duchy of Lancaster, a separately managed collection of estates — and jurisdictions too (the Duchy still appoints magistrates), mainly in the North West. As with Cornwall, this duchy also has a variety of landed estates; some of the holdings can trace their history back through the

Queen has approved the assiduous use (by Lancastrians at home or at gatherings elsewhere throughout the world) of the traditional words with which she is toasted as 'The Queen, Duke of Lancaster'.

'Keeper of the Privy Purse' is, to this day, the title of the Queen's Treasurer, the person responsible for financial org-

The long walk leading to Windsor Castle, one of the Royal houses which belong to the State.

centuries to the days when John of Gaunt's son came to the throne as King Henry IV. Even at that time, Lancaster had become a County Palatine; and the modern county is still Duchy heartland, though new counties of Greater Manchester and Merseyside have been carved from it.

The county name does not figure amongst Her Majesty's official styles, but the

anisation, head of one of the main departments at Buckingham Palace — and who also, incidentally, is Receiver-General for the Duchy of 'time-honoured Lancaster'.

'Privy', however, does not mean 'private'. So Her Majesty's *personal* wealth is not his to know and declare. The Queen's own money — inherited, invested, banked bestowed, or whatever — is as private as anyone else's.

ELIZABETH R

Over the years a number of films and documentaries have focused on members of the Royal Family and aspects of their lives. Edward Mirzoeff, producer and director of BBC TV's Elizabeth R, writes about the making of this latest film to look behind the scenes of the British monarchy.

Only one film had ever been made depicting the life of the Queen. It was "Royal Family", produced by Richard Cawston, and first transmitted on television in June 1969, to an audience of 23 million. It is widely believed to have transformed the

makers were approached; I was the one lucky enough to be chosen.

There were good omens. The sound recordist was to be Peter Edwards, who had done the very same job on "Royal Family"; the film cameraman Philip Bonham-Carter, who

Evenings known as a "Dine and Sleep" at Windsor Castle end with carefully selected 'exhibitions' in the library for guests.

popular image of the monarchy. To this day, everyone remembers the barbecue which the young family enjoyed at Balmoral — nothing so informal to do with royalty had been seen before.

By the summer of 1990 a handful of people in Buckingham Palace and the BBC wondered if the time had come for special access to be given for a second film. The idea — to portray in some detail the working life of the monarch today. The occasion would be the 40th Anniversary of the Queen's accession to the throne, on 6th February 1992. Some distinguished documentary-

had been the assistant cameraman on Cawston's film. Between them they had many years experience of filming at the Palace. And I had a couple of notions how we might approach the project stylistically. First of all, this was to be true documentary — everything filmed as it actually happened, nothing "set up", nothing repeated for the camera. I could not ask the Queen to be an actress.

Second, I wanted to minimize the paraphernalia. Wherever possible we should use no film lighting, or as little as we could get away with; no trailing wires or bulky equipment; and as few of us ourselves

The 1969 documentary "Royal Family" transformed the popular image of the monarchy.

around as was practicable. Our aim was to achieve trust and relaxed intimacy — and that we could gain only by being light on our feet and inconspicuous. Finally, it seemed to me that this film should use little or no archive material — that it would have its value as a record of today, rather than the story of "forty glorious years".

What should we film? What, indeed, would we be allowed to film? It quickly emerged that it was all a matter for negotiation. My counterpart was Charles Anson, the newly-appointed Press Secretary, who in turn would, of course, have to obtain the agreement of The Queen. Her Private Secretary, Sir Robert Fellowes, Deputy Private Secretary, Sir Kenneth Scott and Assistant Private Secretary, Mr Robin Janvrin, would be much involved in all these discussions.

First we looked through the diary of forthcoming public engagements, from the State Opening of Parliament onwards

Sandringham, Windsor, Holyroodhouse and Balmoral — and on the Royal Train, the Queen's Flight, and HMY Britannia.

It was clear to me from the beginning that public engagements could be only a part of our film. They were the familiar side of the Queen's life, seen daily on countless national and regional news bulletins. But what went into the planning and preparation of such events? The

"Elizabeth R" proved to be a fascinating illustration of the varied components of the Queen's life.

through the year. Highlights included a planned State visit to the USA, the Queen's third official visit and her first to Florida and Texas; I quickly expressed interest in that! There was to be a Commonwealth Heads of Government Conference too, in Zimbabwe. A full range of activities in Buckingham Palace, from private audiences to the grandest receptions, would climax in the G7 Heads of Government Summit in July. There were events and occasions to film in all the Queen's residences —

reconnaisance visits, the discussions, the briefings, the homework — surely, I felt, that was where much of the fascination would lie. One of the earliest sequences we filmed was a planning meeting between the Queen and her Private Secretary, Sir Robert Fellowes, looking through the text of her forthcoming Christmas Broadcast. As Sir Robert, pointing out the "Churchillian" adjectives, gracefully suggested slight amendments, and as the Queen responded that at least they had managed to mention

"Elizabeth R" portrayed many aspects of the Queen's working life, including her regular meetings with the Prime Minister.

Christmas, I felt I might be right ....

Luck plays a part in any film. It was our good luck to film a portrait sitting in the small Regency Room in Buckingham Palace on a day when there was a thick blanket of snow in the garden outside. We seemed cut off from the world beyond the walls, no sound of traffic could be heard, and the light reflected from the snow had a soft, gentle luminosity. The Queen seemed at her most

on the tarmac to be allowed aboard ....

We filmed for many hours over the year, and much has inevitably had to be shortened or cut altogether. How sad that there was no room finally for the Queen's visit to her handbag factory, Launer; for a Private Lunch in Buckingham Palace with Nick Faldo and Gillian Lynne among the guests; for the Thistle Ceremony in Edinburgh, which had never been filmed before.

The Queen in a particularly relaxed mood, sitting for her portrait and chatting to artist Andrew Festing.

relaxed, and the artist, Andrew Festing, was a perfect foil. The three of us privileged to be filming that morning knew that there was magic in the air.

We were lucky, too, in the choice of our stills photographer, David Secombe. Not just because of his special documentary talent, but also because of an extra gift for comic mishaps that endeared him to all. Only David could have left a vital part of his camera somewhere in Britannia when she put to sea; only David could have managed to miss Concorde — which flew off from Tampa, Florida with the Queen, the Royal Household and the film crew, but without David Secombe, who was still vainly pleading

But so much else remains that I still find extraordinarily illuminating, instructive, sometimes funny, even touching, in spite of running it backwards and forwards in the cutting-room daily for the past five months. I hope that "Elizabeth R" (a title I decided on quite late — the working title for the film was "Monarchy") provides a true portrait of the Queen's job, and will add to the public understanding of the role of the constitutional monarch today.

My favourite sequence? For a number of reasons, it has to be the Gillies Ball in Balmoral. And the sequence I most regret not filming? There is one — but I'm not going to tell you what it is .....

The BBC is proud to have reported,
reflected and recorded
40 years of service to the nation

BROADCASTING AT ITS BEST

THE ROYAL HOUSEHOLD

The Royal Household is the generic term for the Households of members of the Royal Family, each one operating separately but leaning to some extent on the Queen's Household. Lt.Col. Sir John Johnston, GCVO, MC, former Comptroller of the Lord Chamberlain's Office outlines the functions of the Queen's Household.

In earlier days the Sovereign travelled a good deal round the country, taking his Household with him. Today the majority of the Queen's Household is based at Buckingham Palace with outposts at other royal palaces and residences, i.e. Windsor Castle, Palace of Holyroodhouse, Sandring-

hold, the Lord Great Chamberlain, the Marquess of Cholmondeley, responsible for the conduct of royal matters in the Palace of Westminster, and the Earl Marshal, the Duke of Norfolk, responsible for organising Coronations, State Funerals and the State Opening of Parliament.

The wedding of the Duke and Duchess of York when the Royal Family and members of the Household gathered to bid farewell to the newlyweds.

ham and Balmoral. Whenever the Queen is in residence, on the Royal Yacht or on an overseas State Visit some of her Household from Buckingham Palace accompany her.

The prime task of the Royal Household is to assist the Queen in carrying out her public duties.

Of the former seven Great Officers of State, there are now only two in the House-

The Great Officers of the Household are the Lord Chamberlain (q.v.), the Lord Steward, Viscount Ridley, and the Master of the House, Lord Somerleyton. The Lord Steward is titular head of the Master of the Household's department, his duties mainly ceremonial, being in attendance on important occasions such as State Banquets. The Master of the Horse is titular head of the Royal Mews whose duties are also ceremonial.

The Lord Chamberlain, the Earl of Airlie, is head of the Royal Household. Ceremonially he is responsible for State Visits, Garden Parties, Royal Weddings and Funerals. He oversees the conduct of business of the Household, implements common procedures and policies, is involved in all the senior appointments of the Household and is Chancellor of the Royal Victorian Order.

The members of the Royal Household, who are paid from the Civil List number only a few hundred. They work in one of six departments, over which the Lord Chamberlain has jurisdiction, departments of the Private Secretary, Keeper of the Privy Purse, Master of the Household, Comptroller Lord Chamberlain's Office, Crown Equerry and Director of the Royal Collection.

The Private Secretary's Office is the senior of the departments in the Household. The Queen has a Private Secretary, Sir Robert Fellowes; a Deputy Private Secretary, Sir Kenneth Scott; and an Assistant Private Secretary, Mr Robin Janvrin. One of these three has almost daily contact with the Queen and they are responsible for Her Majesty's programme and the majority of her engagements.

The office informs and advises the Queen on constitutional, governmental and political matters in the UK and Commonwealth, including communications with the Prime Minister and Government departments in all her Realms.

It deals with the majority of the Queen's correspondence, helped by a Lady in Waiting (q.v.). The Private Secretary looks after the Queen's speeches and messages, including those of congratulation to centenarians and couples celebrating their diamond wedding.

The office is also responsible for arrangements concerning the Royal Yacht and the Queen's Flight. On Service matters help is provided by the Defence Services Secretary, currently Major General Brian Pennicott, an appointment filled by the three Services in turn.

The Press Office at Buckingham Palace is part of the Private Secretary's office. The Queen has a Press Secretary, Mr Charles Anson; a Deputy Press Secretary, Mr John Haslam, and two Assistant Press Secretaries, Mr Richard Arbiter and Mr Geoffrey Crawford. They deal with all press, broadcasting and related matters on behalf of the Queen, the Duke of Edinburgh and immediate members of the Royal Family, including press facilities at public engagements at home and abroad.

The Private Secretary is also Keeper of the Royal Archives, which consists mainly of the personal and official correspondence of former Sovereigns and other members of the Royal Family.

Sir Shane Blewitt is both Keeper of the Privy Purse and Treasurer to the Queen. He manages the Sovereign's financial affairs and those of the Household, Private Estates, Racing Establishments and Studs and is responsible for housing and liaison with the other Royal Households on financial matters.

As Treasurer he controls and accounts for

Lt. Col Sir John Miller, who as Crown Equerry from 1961-1989, was in charge of the Royal Mews.

expenditure of the Civil List, the money allocated by the Government to finance the Queen as Head of State, the majority of which is spent on salaries of the working Household.

The Privy Purse receives its income from the Duchy of Lancaster to pay for the semi-official and private expenditure of the Queen incurred as Head of State.

The Office is responsible for presenting

certain parts of royal palaces and residences to the public and other royal enterprises. All personnel matters of employees are dealt with in this department.

The majority of the Civil List employees work in the Master of the Household's Department. The Master of the Household, Rear Admiral Sir Paul Greening, with his Deputy, Lt.Col. Blair Stewart-Wilson, is responsible for the staff, domestic and maintenance arrangements in all royal palaces and royal residences.

The Master of the Household has the responsibility for the catering and entertaining, official and private, in all royal palaces and residences and on HMY

Department of the Metropolitan Police help with security arrangements at the royal palaces.

The Court Post Office is another of the responsibilities of The Master of the Household. He himself is Chairman of the Board of Green Cloth, an institution dating from Tudor times which grants licences to clubs and public houses in the environs of Buckingham Palace.

The Lord Chamberlain's Office is a department in its own right and is headed by the Comptroller, Lt.Col. Malcolm Ross. He is helped by an Assistant Comptroller, Lt.Col. Anthony Mather, who is also the Secretary of the Central Chancery of the

The stables in the Royal Mews, a 'village' within Buckingham Palace. The buildings were designed by John Nash.

Britannia which can range from a Garden Party for 8000 guests to a private lunch for eight.

The department is divided into three branches. In 'F' are the chefs and their helpers and the clerical staff who order the food, kitchen equipment, etc. In 'G' are the Palace Steward, Pages, Yeomen of Pantries and the Royal Cellars, Under Butlers, Footmen and Maintenance and Garden Staff. In 'H' are the Housekeeper, Maids and Cleaners.

The Royalty and Diplomatic Protection

Order of Knighthood, which administers the different Orders of Chivalry.

The Comptroller's principal duties are to make arrangements for incoming State Visits, Investitures, Presentation of Credentials by newly appointed High Commissioners and Ambassadors, Garden Parties and other engagements of the Queen delegated by the Private Secretary.

The Comptroller plays an official role at the State Opening of Parliament and also has the happy duty of arranging Royal weddings and the sad one of arranging Royal funerals. The Office advises on matters of precedence and Royal protocol.

The Royal Mews is a village community made up of chauffeurs, coachmen, grooms, and farriers. It houses the carriage horses, coaches and motor cars and is administered by The Crown Equerry, Lt.Col. Seymour Gilbort-Denham.

Its fine buildings, located in the South-West corner of Buckingham Palace, were designed by John Nash. Built around a quadrangle, they are open to the public at certain times of the year.

The Crown Equerry is responsible for the provision of carriage processions for major

three sections.

It is a unique collection brought together over many years by successive Sovereigns, each introducing his or her personal taste. Much of it is on public display in the state apartments of Palaces, and there are changing exhibitions in the Queen's Gallery, Buckingham Palace. The Queen is generous in lending items from the Collection to exhibitions.

The Surveyor of Pictures, Mr Christopher Lloyd, has over 17,000 paintings and miniatures in his care. By many well known artists, they include some superb works by Canaletto, Gainsborough and Van Dyck — to name but a few.

Lady Susan Hussey, Lady-in-Waiting to the Queen, the Countess of Airlie, Lady of the Bedchamber, Sir William Heseltine, former Private Secretary and Sir Robert Fellowes, Private Secretary since 1990.

ceremonial occasions, and for the fleet of cars used by the Queen, the immediate members of her family and by members of the Household on official engagements. He also provides riding horses and ponies for the Royal Family.

Formed in 1987 the main offices of the Royal Collection Department are situated at St. James's Palace and Windsor Castle. The department has three sections under the control of the Surveyor of Pictures, the Surveyor of Works of Art and the Librarian. Its Director, Sir Geoffrey de Bellaigne, is responsible for all components of the Royal Collection, co-ordinating the work of the

The Surveyor of Works of Art, Sir Geoffrey de Bellaigne, and his Deputy, Mr Hugh Roberts, have similar responsibilities relating to a wide field of works of art — furniture, porcelain (particularly Sevres), jewellery (notably Fabergé), glass, clocks, armour etc.

The Librarian, Mr Oliver Everett, is responsible for the Royal Library at Windsor Castle which contains many early books such as the Mainz Psalter, only the second book to be printed with movable type.

Conservation of the Royal Collection is a heavy responsibility and a mammoth task for the Director and his team. Pictures are cleaned and restored in a studio at St. James's Palace, furniture and armour in workshops at Marlborough House. At Windsor Castle there is a studio for the restoration of drawings and watercolours and books are repaired and rebound in the Royal Bindery.

Alongside, but not in one of the Departments, are the Ladies in Waiting and Equerries. The holders of these appointments fill an indispensable role in the Queen's working life. The ladies are the Mistress of the Robes and Ladies and Women of the Bedchamber. The Mistress of

Wilson, and the other, currently Wing Commander David Walker, being appointed from the three services in turn for a period of three years. The Equerry in Waiting is in attendance on the Queen on all public engagements and also makes some of her private arrangements. There is also a Temporary Equerry from the Coldstream Guards, Captain Julian Giles, who helps out when required. There are also about thirty Extra Equerries, mostly past and present members of the Household. The post is an honorary one and they are rarely called upon for duty.

This then is the working Household, a

The Queen's Private Secretary and Keeper of the Queen's Archives, Sir Robert Fellowes, at RAF Benson, the headquarters of The Queen's Flight.

the Robes, the Duchess of Grafton, attends Her Majesty on state occasions, some overseas State Visits and selected home engagements. Of the Ladies of the Bedchamber, the Countess of Airlie and Lady Farnham, one is in attendance on joint engagements of the Queen and the Duke of Edinburgh. The four Women of the Bedchamber are in waiting for two weeks at a time, attending the Queen on engagements and helping with correspondence.

The Queen has two Equerries, the permanent one being the Deputy Master of the Household, Lt.Col. Blair Stewart-

group of individuals with different talents and from varying backgrounds, each one dedicated to serving the Queen.

At one time the Lord Chamberlain, the Lord Steward and the Mistress of the Robes — amongst others — were political appointments. Nowadays the Captain of the two Body Guards and some of the Lords or Baronesses in Waiting are selected from the Government Whips in the House of Lords. From the Whips Office in the House of Commons are nominated the Treasurer, Comptroller and Vice-Chamberlain of the Household.

EXCELLENCE

Rolls-Royce plc congratulates Her Majesty Queen Elizabeth II on the 40th anniversary of her accession. We are proud to say that our values are the same as those which have set the nation such a constant example.

ROLLS-ROYCE plc, 65 BUCKINGHAM GATE, LONDON SW1E 6AT.

ROYAL TRANSPORT

The Queen and her family spend large periods of time travelling, both at home and abroad. A fleet of vehicles is available to transport them as quickly and efficiently as possible. Andrew Pastouna, author of "The Royal Rolls-Royce Motor Cars" (Osprey) chronicles the history of the Royal motor car.

The provision of suitable transport for the British monarch has always been an important part of the panalopy of Majesty. The first Queen Elizabeth used what today would be regarded as a carriage. British coachbuilding skills then ensured that the Royal family always enjoyed the most comfortable and impressive conveyances. Until the close of Queen Victoria's reign these were entirely horse-drawn, but in 1900 her eldest son introduced the motor car into his household. Shortly after his reign as Edward VII began the State motor car made its introduction.

It was the Coventry motor manufacturer Daimler that Edward VII patronised for his official vehicles. They provided the chassis, and the established coachbuilder Hooper & Co provided the bodywork. Whilst the King patronised Hoopers, the Queen sought out one of the other great coachbuilders, H J Mulliner. These two companies were to maintain links with the Court for over eighty years.

For over half a century the public had become accustomed to viewing their monarch acknowledging the crowds from behind the fluted radiator of the mighty Daimler. It was only upon the accession of Queen Elizabeth II in 1952 that this situation changed.

George VI was reputed to have said that he thought Rolls-Royce produced very fine motor cars for industrialists, whilst Daimler provided transport for the gentlemen. Whatever his views and those of his predecessors,

The No.1 State car — a Jubilee gift to the Queen in 1978.

his brothers, the Dukes of Windsor, Gloucester and Kent and his sister, the Princess Royal, all owned Rolls-Royce cars.

In November 1947 Prince Philip married Princess Elizabeth. Amongst the many wedding gifts was a Daimler limousine, purchased out of funds raised by the RAF and WAAF. But the Daimler tradition was about to be usurped.

In 1948 the young Prince paid a visit to Rolls-Royce where he saw an experimental straight-eight engined Bentley. After driving the car he asked if he could borrow it for a short while. This 100mph vehicle had such accelerative powers that it even worried the development engineers, and they were relieved to get the car back and without incident.

That same year Prince Philip enquired of Rolls-Royce if they could consider producing a special car for the Princess and himself. At this time Rolls-Royce were only producing six-cylinder engines for civil use, and the experimental Bentley had utilised an engine designed for military use. By coincidence the Foreign Office had recently approached the company to provide three cars for General Franco. He insisted on heavily armour protected vehicles, which Rolls-Royce considered would impose a burden on the six cylinder engine. With four orders guaranteed, Rolls-Royce decided to launch the Phantom IV model using the straight eight engine which would only be available to Heads of State.

The car was to change the shape of Royal motoring. Delivered in July 1950, for

BY APPOINTMENT TO
HER MAJESTY QUEEN ELIZABETH II
MOTOR CAR MANUFACTURERS
ROLLS-ROYCE MOTOR CARS LIMITED

CONGRATULATIONS TO HER MAJESTY ON FORTY HAPPY AND GLORIOUS YEARS.

Rolls Royce Motor Cars Limited. A Vickers Company.

the next year and half it was seen on all the principal engagements of the Royal couple. At Buckingham Palace the King and Queen remained faithful to Daimler, having taken delivery of two new State cars the previous year.

Queen Elizabeth II undertook no official engagements for the first two months of her reign. The first time she was seen after the funeral of the King was the traditional Maundy service held at Westminster Abbey on April the 10th.

It had been decided that the Rolls-Royce Phantom IV was to be painted in the Royal colours, claret over black, and that it's number plates would be removed making it

---

THE QUEEN'S FLIGHT

Five aircraft and about one hundred and eighty officers and men of the Royal Air Force make up one of the world's most remarkable flying units — The Queen's Flight.

The Queen's Flight provides air transport for the Queen, members of the Royal Family, visiting Heads of State, the Prime Minister, certain Senior Ministers, the Chiefs of Staff and other VIPs. Its origins can be traced back to flights in 1917 and 1918 by the Prince of Wales and Prince Albert. The Prince of Wales bought and operated several aircraft privately, but it was not until 21st July 1936 that The King's Flight was officially formed at Hendon.

The Flight moved to RAF Benson, some 40 miles west of London, in September 1939. On 1st August 1952, following the accession of the Queen, the Flight was renamed The Queen's Flight and between 1955 and 1961 its four Vickers Vikings were replaced by de Havilland Herons.

In 1959 two Westland Whirlwind helicopters joined the Flight on a perm-anent basis. The Flight now operates three BAe 146 and two Wessex helicopters.

During the early 1950's there were about 60 Royal Flights each year, but from 1954 when the helicopters began to be used, this total has increased to some 1200 a year, of which half are by helicopter.

Because of the limited range of the BAe 146 some very long range flights for major Royal visits overseas are undertaken by RAF transport aircraft or civil aircraft on charter under supervision of The Queen's Flight. On these occasions a BAe 146 is often positioned overseas to fly the Queen from small airfields in the country concerned.

The present Captain of The Queen's Flight is Air Commodore the Hon. T C Elworthy CBE who acts as adviser to the Queen on all aspects of Royal flying.

To assist him there are two Deputy Captains, five BAe 146 crews and three helicopter crews — one of the Wessex pilots being an officer from the Royal Navy. The Duke of Edinburgh and The Prince of Wales, as qualified pilots, often fly the aircraft themselves.

For flights in British airspace, air traffic control lanes known as Purple Airways and

An aircraft from The Queen's Flight based at RAF Benson.

Royal Low Level Corridors are established which enable special arrangements to be made for separating Royal aircraft from other air traffic.

All the aircraft of The Queen's Flight are painted in a distinctive red, white and blue livery and when on the ground they fly the Personal Standard of the member of The Royal Family on board.

All the aircraft are maintained to an exceptionally high standard and conse-quently their record of reliability is second to none. This record is due entirely to the skill and dedication of the air and ground crews — all of whom are volunteers.

ROYAL YACHT BRITANNIA

The Royal Yacht Britannia is both an official and private residence for the Queen and members of the Royal Family, usually during visits overseas, but at times in home waters.

When the Queen launched the Britannia on Clydebank in 1953 she stressed that the Royal yacht was not a pleasure boat but a Royal palace-at-sea. Britannia, built at a cost of £2,098,000 replaced the Victoria and Albert III which

Interconnecting lounges on the Royal Yacht Britannia.

had served three sovereigns since being built in 1901.

Both the Queen and Prince Philip took a keen interest in the design and fitting out of the ship and after looking at various possibilities, commissioned Sir Hugh Casson to undertake the design of the rooms. Sir Hugh's simple and unfussy designs incorporated some of the furniture and fittings transferred from the Victoria and Albert III. Over the years gifts and souvenirs from overseas trips have been added.

As well as the royal apartments, accommodation on board the ship includes berths for the crew as well as offices and a reception room which can cater for up to 250 guests. The State apartments are often used by the Queen and the Royal Family when visiting foreign countries allowing them to reciprocate hospitality on foreign shores.

Britannia has also been brought into service in recent years for the holding of business seminars on board, known as "Sea Days". Primarily to promote British and Commonwealth trade overseas, these seminars allow industrialists and financiers to meet their foreign counterparts. Results for British exports have been excellent with many millions of pounds of business generated so far.

Twenty-one officers and 229 men make up the ship's company, all of whom are volunteers within the Navy, which is under the command of the Flag Officer Royal Yachts. Normally appointed for a period of five years, the Britannia is currently under the command of Rear-Adm. Robert Woodard. As the only Admiral in the Navy who is also Captain of a ship he is a member of the Royal Household and responsible for the day-to-day activities of the ship.

Royal Yachtsmen wear a customised uniform similar to the regular naval dress but with the jumper tucked inside the trousers, which are finished at the top with a black silk bow. Uniform badges are white instead of the customary red.

On all major tours a Royal Marines Band accompanies the Royal Family and perform orchestral, ceremonial and concert military band functions. They are regularly seen performing the traditional ceremony of Beat Retreat.

Britannia has now travelled nearly one million miles, visited every continent and the majority of Commonwealth countries. Not only has she been a floating palace and home from home but been used in a successful and profitable manner to promote British and Commonwealth interests worldwide.

the number one State car. On that April morning the gates at Clarence House swung open to allow the new monarch in her Rolls-Royce to depart on the first public engagement of the new Elizabethan age.

It was to be another eight years before the last of King George's State Daimler's left

the Royal Mews.

Meanwhile Rolls-Royce decided as a speculative idea to build a State car based on the landaulette coachwork design with bodywork by the Royal coachbuilders Hooper & Co. This was loaned to the Palace from 1954 until 1959 when it was decided to purchase the vehicle. It had also been agreed that a new Phantom V State car would be built in 1960 to be followed by another a year later.

With transparent roofs over the rear compartment and full air conditioning, they revolutionised State transport as much as the earlier Phantom IV.

In 1978 Her Majesty accepted as a Jubilee gift from the Society of Motor Manufacturing and Traders, a brand New Phantom VI as her number one State car. In 1987 the Phantom IV Hooper landaulette was retired and replaced with a standard body Phantom VI. However, the Royal Mews still maintains the first 1950 Phantom

IV which seems to be much favoured by the Princess of Wales.

Not every road journey by the Head of State is in a State car, however, for personal use the Queen has used a Daimler saloon, Rovers, a Jaguar saloon, and a Vauxhall Brake. As with her State vehicles the Queen keeps them a long time, ten years each at least for her private cars, some even longer, whilst her Rolls-Royce models are between 5 and 42 years old. How many families can claim that sort of longevity? It is more than certain that the present Rolls-Royces will last well past the Golden Jubilee in 2002.

THE ROYAL TRAIN

Royal trains in some form have been in use by the Royal Family for over 150 years.

It was in 1977 to mark the Queen's Silver Jubilee that the current Royal Train came into service but Royal trains of some description have been in use since 1840. The very first was, in fact, a coach built by the Great Western Railway Company but it was two years before the then Queen, Victoria, tested out the railway, and only after modifications had taken place to make the coach safer. This very first Royal train journey was from Slough to Paddington and took twenty-five minutes.

Today the Royal Train is used by all the Royal Family as a quick and efficient method of travelling between official functions. There is no Royal Train as such, but a series of carriages all with specific uses which are pulled by a standard British Rail engine. The Royal Saloons, of which there are two, were standard Inter-City passenger saloons adapted to meet the specific needs of royal travellers, with furniture and fittings personally chosen by the Queen and the Duke of Edinburgh. The President of the Royal Academy of Art, Sir Hugh Casson, was an advisor on the interior design as was the Director of Industrial Design for the British Railways Board.

The Queen's Saloon has four main areas, a formal entrance vestibule, a sitting room, a bedroom and bathroom. It connects to a second bedroom, bathroom and vestibule. This is similar to the layout of the Duke of

Edinburgh's saloon but this also includes a kitchen which can cater for ten people.

Past British Sovereigns have been enthusiastic train travellers and some of

The Royal Train consists of a collection of specially adapted passenger saloons pulled by a standard engine.

the carriages used by previous monarchs can be seen at the National Railway Museum in York. The current fleet of carriages were updated in 1985 with eight new vehicles converted from new or surplus stock and two new carriages added.

A tradition of excellent taste.

Mattessons Wall's Ltd. congratulate Her Majesty The Queen on the occasion of the 40th anniversary of her reign.

State and Royal Occasions

Robert Hudson reports on his experiences as a commentator for many Royal occasions, including the funeral of Sir Winston Churchill, the Silver Jubilee, the State Opening of Parliament, Trooping the Colour and three Royal Weddings.

"Will Her Majesty know that the microphones are being carried out to the dais by a sergeant in the Welsh Guards?" My tentative question was addressed to the formidable figure of The Earl Marshal, The Duke of Norfolk. "The Queen", he replied, and I was glad to note a twinkle in his eyes, "will know everything." And so it was and always is.

That brief exchange took place at a meeting in London to finalise Broadcasting and Press arrangements for the Investiture of the Prince of Wales at Caernarvon on 1st July 1969.

As this was to be a State Occasion, the Duke as Earl Marshal was in charge of the organisation.

As Head of Outside Broadcasts, I was responsible for world-wide radio coverage for the BBC. We both had our problems.

Mine were concerned with fitting modern technology, commentators and engineers into an ancient castle; the Earl Marshal's with questions of protocol, security, timing and, not least, I imagine, with briefing the Queen, Prince Philip and Prince Charles about a ceremony which had not taken place for fifty-eight years. Even then, in 1911, it was carried out, also at Caernarvon Castle, in a green and white

1969 — The first investiture of a Prince of Wales for 58 years.

tent out of public view.

Now it was to be a television spectacular, masterminded by Lord Snowdon, in his role as Constable of the Castle, and carried out by Antony Craxton, the BBC producer.

The Queen's infallible ability to do the right thing does not arise only from her long experience. Some events are hardy annuals and present no great difficulty — a minor change here and there, perhaps. Others are 'one-offs'; for these the briefing must match the perfect organisation we have come to take for granted in Britain.

As with most State and Royal Occasions, there was no complete rehearsal of the whole Investiture Ceremony.

The procedure on the slate dais, with its four steps and perspex roof, was rehearsed, with bits of string as guidelines, on the flat lawns of Buckingham Palace. Orchestras, choirs, bands and trumpeters all went through their paces separately, as did the processions inside and outside the castle. For my part, I made sure that Sergeant Reeves practised carrying the microphones to a spot, marked by a small piece of tape, on the dais. This was just as well because, at rehearsal, he did this with such military enthusiasm that the cable came out of its socket.

Meanwhile, I had arranged for a true Welshman, Alun Williams, to give the main commentary (in English) from the top of the Chamberlain's Tower. Others,

Music of the Household Division, and an old friend of mine, had his problems as well, with a scattered ensemble of bands and trumpeters, dotted round the walls. When the Queen presented Prince Charles to the people outside the castle, at Queen

The State Opening of Parliament — the only annual State event.

broadcasting in Welsh, were stationed on the battlements below. Fifteen other commentators, from the BBC's Overseas Services, and from foreign broadcasting organisations, were strung along the ramparts, each with a television monitor screen to let them see round corners. Our engineers, rather to their dismay, were consigned to a dungeon.

Visual control, of the 'mixing' of sound and speech, was essential and we were lucky to find a window, in the Black Tower, which overlooked the dais. From here music, speech and sound effects were 'fed' in, as is the normal practice on big occasions, by BBC radio to our own television service and to all other organisations taking the programme. Each Service would add its own commentaries separately.

Lt. Colonel Jaeger, Senior Director of

Eleanor's Gate, a second conductor was stationed on the roof of the Post Office, so that the trumpeters could face outwards!

The activities of the Welsh Nationalists caused elaborate security arrangements to be made. I, myself, returned to London on the morning of the Investiture, to take my place in the continuity suite at Broadcasting House, in case some disaster occurred at Caernarvon and programme changes were needed. My able deputy, Arthur Phillips, was left to produce the live programme, and the edited version later in the day.

It was with some relief that I heard Raymond Baxter, in Caernarvon Square, describe the safe arrival of the processions from the Royal Train, halted about two miles away. Soon we had a Prince of Wales duly invested who, in response to the Loyal Address, spoke in excellent Welsh. The music and singing, at which of course the

Welsh excel, and the tumultuous reception given to the new Prince of Wales, made it a wonderful day and a fine broadcast. What is more, the vermilion-coloured chairs, used by spectators in the castle, were all sold for £12 each!

Earl Marshal and the Lord Great Chamberlain, who confided to me, in an interview, that he only kept his bearings by squinting downwards at the black shoes of the Yeomen of the Guard, who line the Royal Gallery.

Trooping the Colour with the Queen riding Burmese, the horse she rode at the ceremony for 18 years.

State Occasions, as such, are comparatively rare. They require not only the presence of the Head of State, the reigning Monarch, but also of Garter King of Arms, the Heralds and the Pursuivants. The only annual example is the State Opening of Parliament, when the full panoply of State is on display. Here, looking like human Court playing cards in their exotic uniforms, 'Rouge Croix Pursuivant' will walk with 'Portcullis', while the 'York' and 'Somerset' Heralds follow behind. They precede the Queen to the House of Lords, just as, centuries ago, they would go ahead to announce the arrival of the Monarch. Meanwhile, dismounted troopers of the Life Guards and Blues and Royals will have lined the staircase leading up to the Robing Room. Here the Queen puts on the Imperial State Crown and the train of her crimson Robe of State is carried by pages. In front of her distinguished persons carry the Cap of Maintenance and the Sword of State — a heavy implement, which proved too much for Field Marshal Montgomery in his declining years. Walking backwards, and facing the Queen, are the

I broadcast the State Opening of Parliament, for BBC Radio, on six occasions. Normally all went well but, in 1974, my commentary box, in the House of Lords, had not been properly soundproofed and my voice could be clearly heard during the silence which ensues while Black Rod sets off down the corridors and through the lobbies to summon the Commons. A member of the Royal Family was reported as saying that it was much more interesting with a commentary!

The radio broadcast has many difficulties, not least that much of it has to be done from the television screen, because only the House of Lords itself is visible to the naked eye. Throughout it all the Queen preserves a supernatural calm and dignity, taking out her spectacles from a small handbag, to read the speech proffered by the Lord Chancellor. Her Majesty has a clear broadcasting voice and rarely, if ever, makes a mistake. At the State Opening, however, angelic qualities are added, because the BBC microphones are attached to the figure of an angel to the right of the throne!

More common than a State Occasion is the Royal Occasion; Royal Weddings, and the Silver Jubilee of 1977. These are organised by the Lord Chamberlain, the head of the Queen's Household. Also, very much a Royal Occasion, is the 'Queen's Birthday Parade', as it is officially called, although most people know it as 'Trooping the Colour'.

I broadcast this for twenty-one successive years for BBC Radio, from a window high up in the Horse Guards Building. During all this time, from 1961 — 81 inclusive, the Queen never missed the Parade. For most of those years she rode, side-saddle, the faithful police horse, Burmese, who also took a keen interest in the proceedings and seemed to move off in the right direction without any prompting from the Queen, an elegant and regal figure in her red uniform, blue sash of the Order of the Garter, black tricorn hat and dark blue habit. Sadly Burmese retired to Windsor in 1986, where she died in 1990, and Her Majesty is now driven onto Horse Guards Parade in a carriage. They must miss each other. Even when blank cartridges were fired, near the Royal Procession, in 1981, Burmese was only momentarily startled and the Queen's fine horsemanship was soon a calming influence.

The Trooping broadcast is long and complicated. It requires a very thorough knowledge of the Parade and much detailed preparation. I always interviewed the key figures, visited the Household Cavalry stables and the Regiment whose colour was being 'trooped'. The music of the Massed Bands is attractive and important. My aim was to let the listener hear all the best of it, without talking over it. This entailed attending the Band rehearsals, as well as the full-scale rehearsals on two Saturdays before the Birthday Parade itself. Despite all the preparation, I was nervous on my first attempt at this marathon, spectacular show-piece event.

"The Guards", I said, "are drawn up in a square rectangle ready to be inspected by the Queen in their bearskins." Now that would have made an interesting picture!

Each year, on Remembrance Sunday, the Armed Forces and the Civilian Services line the roadway on either side of Whitehall. Massed Bands fill the road to the south and veterans of the British Legion to the north. At exactly 10.59 Her Majesty the Queen, Prince Philip and other male members of the Royal Family leave the Home Office building, to stand, facing the Cenotaph, for the two minutes' silence, to lay their wreaths, and to take part in the short service which follows.

I broadcast the Ceremony at the Cenotaph on twenty-one occasions.

Each year I felt an acute sense of responsibility towards tens of thousands of listeners, all over the world, who had lost a loved one in either of the two wars, or, perhaps, in one of the conflicts since. In my mind's eye I saw three friends of mine at school, none of whom reached his twenty-first birthday; one killed in Sicily, one drowned at sea, the third shot down in the Battle of Britain. I thought, too, of my own colleagues in the army, who were killed in action.

What makes this broadcast so uniquely difficult is that it combines split-second timing, especially in the final minute before the Silence, with a very strong feeling of emotion. It is a broadcast in which every word must drop precisely into place and in which the commentator must strike exactly the right note. The mood changes from the martial to the wistful and solemn; from "Rule Britannia" to "Nimrod". Then the Silence — with only the rumble of distant traffic to remind us that we don't all stop, as we used to do, to remember the one-and-three-quarter million who died. Finally, after the National Anthem comes the march past of the British Legion — more than ever last year — to the old familiar tunes of "Tipperary", "Pack up your Troubles", "There'll always be an England".

At the Cenotaph, the Queen stands quite alone, the Royal Princes behind her. There is no bodyguard, no bullet-proof glass. We don't do things that way. As she steps forward to lay her wreath of red poppies, she does so on behalf of the nation. The row of politicians await their turn. In one glance we see a Democratic Government, under a Constitutional Monarchy, paying homage to those who died to keep it so.

State and Royal Occasions provide rare opportunities for displays of national unity. They preserve our history and our heritage in an unique manner, unrivalled anywhere in the world.

At all these events, over the last forty years, Her Majesty and Prince Philip have combined the essential mystique of the Monarchy with stability, commonsense and good humour. We should be profoundly grateful.

The Queen stands alone at the Cenotaph paying homage to the dead of two World Wars.

P.O. Box N 752
Nassau
Bahamas.
Tel (809) 393-5366

The Nassau Yacht Club extends loyal greetings to Her Majesty Queen Elizabeth II on the 40th Anniversary of her reign.

We recall with pleasure Her Majesty's many visits to the Commonwealth of the Bahamas with His Royal Highness the Duke of Edinburgh and on the occasion of his sailing in Montagu Bay.

It is perhaps fitting, in this the Quincentennial Anniversary of Christopher Columbus' discovery of the Bahamas, that The Duke of Edinburgh Trophy, presented to this Club by His Royal Highness in 1960, will again be sailed in competition when we host the International 5.5 Metre Class races in April 1992.

The Commodore, Officers and Members of the Nassau Yacht Club send heartiest congratulations and wish Her Majesty long life and good health.

Ivy C. French
Commodore

TRAVELS WITH THE QUEEN

As the most travelled monarch in world history, there are few countries which the Queen has not visited. Tom Corby, Press Association Court Correspondent since 1985 has experienced first hand the organisation, skills and hard work which go into a Royal Tour.

The brass bound trunks and cases stand like sentry boxes in the corridors of Buckingham Palace, each one emblazoned "The Queen" in gold lettering.

The score or so of upright hanging trunks contain enough clothes for two or three changes a day, hats, jewellery, and the occasional tiara. But carefully packed also is a plentiful supply of Malvern water, a specially selected blend of Early Grey tea, an electric kettle, marmalade, shortbread biscuits, Dundee cake and peppermint creams.

Her Majesty Queen Elizabeth II, roving ambassador extraordinaire, is about to go on her travels again.

The Queen is in fact the most travelled monarch in world history, and there are few countries she has not visited in her official capacity. She has walked the Great Wall of China, where the citizens of the People's Republic greeted her as "the English Female King", addressed a joint meeting of the United States Congress, and has met virtually all the world's leaders, some still in their positions of power, some with desirable reputations, others with less so, a few now deposed or having died in mysterious circumstances.

She has made three State Visits to America, the last in May 1991, to re-affirm the solidarity of Anglo-US relations in the

King George VI with Princess Elizabeth and Princess Margaret on a tour of South Africa in 1947.

wake of the successful conclusion of the Gulf War, and in Spain, in 1988, she did much to placate Iberian sensibilities over the sovereignty of Gibraltar, ceded to Britain by the Treaty of Utrecht in the reign of Queen Anne.

As Head of the Commonwealth she has visited all the Commonwealth countries: 16 times to Canada and 12 times to Australia, for instance. She was in Kenya on the first stage of a tour to Sri Lanka, Australia and New Zealand, at the time of her accession to the throne on the death of her father, King George VI, on February 6 1952.

Along the way she has endured extremes of heat and cold; had eggs thrown at her in New Zealand, been shouted at by French separatists in Canada, and been virtually abandoned in a desert tent by a capricious King. But invariably as she progressed round the world she has been cheered, applauded, hugged, and even kissed by excited admirers.

And she has been called upon in the course of duty to eat and drink some very strange mixtures indeed. In China she dined on sea slug and dragon eyes while the Military Band of the Chinese People's Liberation Army played Greensleeves, and in tiny Belize was served something akin to a rat, roasted maskall gibnut, which, she was assured, was a local delicacy.

A royal tour, as anyone who has ever been

on one knows, is no holiday. But the benefits to Britain, in terms of boosted trade, the smoothing of diplomatic relations, and the sheer good will generated, defy calculation.

There is simply no better way to understand and appreciate the Royal Family's influence than to travel with them. A tour

On the world tour of 1954 the Queen waves from a train in New Zealand.

confronts people in other countries with an idea of Britain that is powerful and a little mysterious; that of a modern, technological democracy, which, despite whingings in the wings by a minority about its cost, has the good sense to retain a Monarchy to give stability and an aura of glamour and mystique other countries lack.

The Queen represents the kind of Britain in which most of us would feel a sense of pride. Her power and trappings are mighty, but her manner is engagingly down to earth. She is the reality of a Monarchy which to outsiders might seem unreal.

Whatever her surroundings, whether in a flower filled canoe somewhere in the Pacific, or encircled by painted African warriors, she somehow manages to give the impression of a Home Counties lady on her way to a wedding. It is very comforting and re-assuring.

The reasons for a royal visit overseas are varied. Sometimes it is a straightforward cementing of good relations, or a return visit after a foreign Head of State has been to Britain and entertained at Buckingham Palace or Windsor Castle.

There are of course specific reasons too. The Queen and Prince Philip's historic visit to China in October 1986 was made against the background of the Joint Declaration on the future of Hong Kong; the Queen's visits to Australia — in 1988 for its bicentennial celebrations — are seen as stemming incipient republicanism there.

This year, for obvious reasons, much of the Queen's travelling concentrates on Europe. She will be addressing the European Parliament in Strasbourg, and also making State Visits to France and Germany, and Malta.

And although at the time it might all seem effortless, months of detailed planning by royal officials, the Foreign Office, and by the host country, go into the smooth running of the Queen on tour overseas.

The first approach is almost always informal. Then once a tentative date is agreed a formal invitation is issued, followed by simultaneous announcements by the Queen's Press Secretary and the host country which submits a series of programmes and alternatives for the Queen's approval.

Dorothy Laird, doyen of royal authors, describes the Queen's attitude perfectly in her book "How The Queen Reigns"; saying "The Queen goes through these plans with the greatest care and she makes many suggestions. She reads a programme as an architect reads plans or a musician an orchestral score."

The Queen does indeed do her homework thoroughly, familiarising herself with the political, parliamentary, and economic background of the country to be visited.

The island of Singapore has received many visits from members of the Royal Family over the years.

PAPUA NEW GUINEA BANKING CORPORATION

It is with great pleasure that I take this opportunity to congratulate Her Majesty Queen Elizabeth II on the Fortieth Anniversary of Her Accession.

This anniversary encompasses national and international dimensions. The example which has been set of public service and duty has been an inspiration to us all. This example has encouraged generations to face the challenges of life whilst working for the public good, to face the future with confidence and above all, to pursue excellence.

The example which has been set to promote understanding and harmony around the world is unique and I hope Her Majesty continues her work for many years to come.

SIR MEKERE MORAUTA

On the 40th anniversary of V E Day in June 1944 the Queen with other Heads of State representing countries involved in WWII.

The climate, the season, and the customs of the country concerned are all considered. The clothes she will take are planned to match climate and provide the comfort and ease she needs to carry out her role effectively. She has, in the past, worn dresses which compliment, in colour and design, the host country; a gown decorated with maple leaves for Canada, for example. Gifts, orders, and signed photographs are chosen for distribution to her hosts and those who will look after her.

If the Queen is to be away for any length of time Counsellors of State are appointed to stand in for her at meetings of the Privy Council, to exercise the functions of the absent Sovereign. Under the Regency Acts, 1937-53, the Queen is empowered to appoint six

Counsellors of State: the Duke of Edinburgh, Queen Elizabeth, the Queen Mother, and the four Princes or Princesses next in line of succession. But in fact only two members of the Royal Family have been appointed in recent years to fulfil this function.

A few weeks before the visit an advance party goes out from Buckingham Palace to liaise with host country officials, and discuss and examine every yard of the proposed royal progress. In Palace parlance this is known as the "recce", and is generally carried out by one of the Queen's Private Secretaries, her Press Secretary, and an officer from the Royalty and Diplomatic Protection Department.

Security is always a major consideration, particularly so now, in these days of threatened terrorist attack, but it is never allowed to interfere unduly with the Queen's philosophy that she must be seen by, and meet, as many people as possible. And indeed be photographed and reported doing it.

This means motocades, frequently in open cars, garden parties, receptions,

Some might argue that one line-up of, say, dancing pineapples, is like any other to the Queen. She has seen it all before. But Her Majesty would not view it that way because the children inside the pineapple costumes represent Commonwealth

The State Visit to Malaysia in 1989 coincided with the Commonwealth Heads of Government meeting in Kuala Lumpur.

dinners, lunches, parades, and huge outdoor rallies for children.

It is the children too, who are paramount, particularly on visits to Commonwealth countries, because it is they who are the future.

continuity. And the children themselves, of course, never forget the occasion they danced before the Queen.

Finally all the planning is distilled between the covers of a handbook which slips

Exchanging gifts with the Amir of Bahrain during a Middle East tour in 1979.

The Port Of Singapore Authority

Congratulates

Her Majesty Queen Elizabeth II

On The 40th Anniversary Of Her

Accession To The Throne.

 **PSA**

SINGAPORE. THE GLOBAL PORT

easily into a pocket or handbag. It details to the minute every part of the visit, from the time of departure from Buckingham Palace or Windsor Castle to the time of touchdown at the Queen's visit to China, for example, she knew that she would be in her car for precisely 10 minutes between Peking's Forbidden City and The Temple of Heaven;

The Queen surrounded by children during a visit to the Children's Palace, Canton in 1986.

Heathrow once the tour is over.

And no member of the entourage can afford to be without it. On the first day of that five minutes was allocated for arriving at the British Embassy, being received by the Ambassador and his wife, planting a tree

Selangor Turf Club

was honoured by the presence of

Her Majesty Queen Elizabeth II

at our

Queen Elizabeth II Commonwealth Cup Race

on

15th October 1989

and

would like to offer

our heartiest congratulations and best wishes

on the 40th anniversary of Her reign as

the Queen of the United Kingdom and Head of the Commonwealth

Dato' Ronald Khoo Teng Swee
Chairman

Selangor Turf Club
Racecourse Jalan Ampang
P.O. Box 10048
50702 Kuala Lumpur
Malaysia

in the garden there, and signing the Visitor's Book.

The Queen was then given a five minute break before meeting 18 Commonwealth

times. For the State Banquet that same night in the Great Hall of the People, the Queen, her ladies in waiting, and other non-Chinese women guests knew that they

Inspecting the troops at the Istana Palace, Singapore.

ambassadors, and having her photograph taken with them. This would take another five minutes. Fifteen minutes was reserved for meeting the staff of the Embassy, and 40 minutes for her attendance at a reception for 600 British and Commonwealth guests in the garden, during which she would invest Flight Lieutenant Ruth Bleasdale, the Embassy Nurse, as an Associate of the Royal Red Cross.

Side notes told the Queen and her suite just what they should be wearing at given

would be in long dresses and (T), for tiara.

The Duke of Edinburgh and the male non-Chinese were, in the egalitarian People's Republic, to be in L.S. — lounge suits.

And so it goes on, day after day, with only a very occasional hitch. Inexplicably, and unusually for a stickler for punctuality, the Queen was five minutes late for the official welcoming ceremony in Tian'anmen Square. The Chinese, who have a high regard for the proprieties, then gauged that

SINGAPORE AIRLINES

WISHES

HER MAJESTY QUEEN ELIZABETH II

CONTINUED GOOD HEALTH

AND HAPPINESS

ON THE 40TH ANNIVERSARY

OF

HER ACCESSION TO THE THRONE

SINGAPORE
AIRLINES

their premier, Zhao Ziyang, would be exactly five minutes late when he arrived to bid the Queen farewell from her Peking guest house!

But the Queen's renowned cool was times she appeared quite baffled by last minute changes in her programme, and at one point was said to have considered leaving a desert tent where she had

The celebrations to mark Australia's bicentenary in 1988 were shared with many members of the Royal Family — the Queen and the Duke of Edinburgh, the Prince and Princess of Wales and the Princess Royal all took part.

never so severely tested than by the erratic behaviour of King Hassan II of Morocco during her State Visit there in 1980. At ostensibly been left alone and neglected for 10 to 15 minutes while the King disappeared into a nearby air conditioned caravan.

Moroccan officials explained that the King had been anxious to check on the arrangements, and ensure all went well, but lunch was served two hours late.

Diplomats said at the time that one had were however rather ruffled when they were ordered out of a room in the guest palace when the King arrived for a lunch.

The King's passion for security manifested itself when he made the Queen

The Queen, the most well travelled monarch in the world, seen here in Iceland during a State Visit in June 1990.

to make allowances for the eccentric King and for the fact that women played a very small part in Moroccan public life.

For the first time ever women were allowed inside the Royal Palace in Rabat because of the Queen's presence there. The Queen's two Ladies in Waiting, the Duchess of Grafton, Mistress of the Robes, and Mrs John Dugdale, change cars seven times on the road from Marrakesh into the foothills of the snowcapped Atlas Mountains. On another occasion, when the King gave a State banquet in the Queen's honour, he suddenly decided to hold it much later than initially planned. The result was that the Queen had to wait in the back of her Rolls Royce for 30

Students cloak the Queen as a sign of respect during a State Visit to Portugal.

CECIL H. GREEN
3525 TURTLE CREEK BOULEVARD
APARTMENT 20-A
DALLAS, TEXAS 75219

PHONE: (214) 526-0812
FAX:(214) 526-2120

"At twenty years of age, the will reigns; at thirty, the wit and at forty, the judgment".

So said Benjamin Franklin talking of life. But surely a monarch needs all three – will, wit and judgment – qualities that have been amply displayed by Her Majesty Queen Elizabeth since 1952.

It is an honour and a privilege to be part of this tribute to the last forty years which have seen many changes in the world and the society in which we live. And yet, steadfast through it all, has been the British Monarchy, a constant in a time of great change.

As the co-founder of Texas Instruments which has been at the forefront of technological development and which continues to lead one of the most dynamic markets over these last four decades, it was a further honour to be made an Honorary Knight of the British Empire in May, 1991.

I have always been proud of my British roots and know that my name will live on with future generations through Green College, Oxford. Indeed, I continue to pursue my interests in the University as Honorary Chairman of the Oxford Campaign in America.

I salute Her Majesty, her work and all that the British Monarchy stands for. Long may she reign.

Cecil H. Green

Cecil H. Green, K.B.E.

minutes in full evening dress and tiara. When an explanation was demanded armed guards at the palace gate said they had not yet received instructions to let the Queen in.

Finally the King excelled himself by arriving 54 minutes late for a banquet being given in his honour by the Queen on board the royal yacht Britannia. The parting of

never know where you are going or when".

When the Queen goes on her travels she takes with her a miniature Royal Household. She will be accompanied by two Private Secretaries, one to keep in touch with the government at home, and with the national and international scene, and advise the Queen accordingly, and another who

The links between Papua New Guinea and the British Crown go back to the 19th century and members of the Royal family have made numerous tours of the country.

the two monarchs two hours later was said to be no more than formal.

Afterwards everyone concerned did their best to smooth things over. The Queen's advisors made the point that she had always known that King Hassan was an eccentric time keeper. The Queen, they said, had always understood this, and was not in the least bit fussed by it.

And the Queen's farewell message to the King from her home bound aircraft was particularly warm. She thanked King Hassan for his "extremely warm and generous hospitality" towards herself and Prince Philip, adding perhaps a trifle ironically "We have been especially touched by the way in which your Majesty took such a personal interest in our programme."

It was the Queen's first visit to Morocco and it was said that she had been told in advance by Princess Margaret that going there was "rather like being kidnapped. You

assumes overall responsibility for the day to day running of the tour.

In addition Her Majesty's Press Secretary will also be in attendance to ensure that the press, both British and foreign, get the information and camera shots they need without being overly intrusive. With sometimes hundreds of media representatives covering a tour of major importance the balance struck can be a delicate one.

If the Queen is making a State Visit she will take with her her equerry, who is a member of the armed forces on temporary secondment, and sometimes her permanent equerry, who is also Deputy Master of the Household. If the visit is to a Commonwealth monarchy an equerry will be appointed by that country for the duration of the visit.

The Foreign Secretary also travels with the Queen on important State Visits — like that to China and to America last summer. The Queen will also have two Ladies in

Waiting with her and a dresser, the Buckingham Palace equivalent of a ladies maid. Prince Philip will take his Private Secretary and a valet. Both the Queen and the Prince will be guarded by their personal protection officers, backed up by a security contingent from the host country.

moments for her. On the Great Wall of China she played tourist as well as royal visitor, emerging from her black Mercedes clutching her Leica camera to stride out in the company of the Mayor of Peking and a mildly perspiring retinue of forty.

She stopped twice in front of a ranked mass

There were three State Visits in 1991, the first in May to the USA where President Bush was host to the Queen.

A reassuring figure in the background, carrying his black bag of emergency medicines is Surgeon Captain Norman Blacklock, the Medical Officer to the Queen abroad. Many a member of the Royal Household has had cause to be grateful for his ministrations, particularly in hot and steamy climes.

The Queen's travels in the 40 years of her reign must have many memorable

of British and Chinese photographers, both still and television, for a pre-arranged pose, and for a photograph which later circled the globe.

Her Majesty, titular head of one quarter of the earth, shared with Ghengis Khan the distinction of having stormed the wall. The Mongol war lord did not however have breakfast television on hand to film the event for posterity.

This statue of Christopher Columbus in front of Government House in Nassau commemorates his 'discovery' of the island in 1492. The Bahamas became independent in 1973 and the Queen and members of the Royal family have toured the islands on several occasions.

ALL THE QUEEN'S HORSES

The Queen is an enthusiastic breeder of horses and takes a keen interest in the animals she owns.
Alan Yuill Walker, author of Thoroughbred Studs of Great Britain (Weidenfeld)
charts the development of the Royal Studs over the last forty years.

One of the pursuits which the Queen likes most is the care and breeding of horses. Indeed, more than an interest and not just a relaxation from the public duties of her office, it is a highly professional business, keenly enjoyed by this Royal racehorse owner.

Sandringham Estate, near King's Lynn in Norfolk, and Polhampton Lodge, between Kingsclere and Highclere, in Hampshire.

The Sovereign has owned and bred the winners of four of the five English classics, with Pall Mall (2000 Guineas), Highclere (1000 Guineas), and Dunfermline (Oaks

The Queen leads her filly Carrozza, ridden by Lester Piggott, into the winners' enclosure after the 1957 Oaks.

It is not merely a matter of Her Majesty's inheritance of the Royal Studs and the Royal Family's love of the Turf, for until the advent of the Arab sheikhs a decade ago, Her Majesty The Queen was one of the country's foremost owner-breeders. Then, as now, she had three breeding establishments, studs at Sandringham and Wolferton on the

and St. Leger). Only the Derby eludes her and, ironically, she sold Height of Fashion, dam of the 1989 Derby winner, Nashwan, to that colt's owner-breeder, Sheikh Hamdan Al Maktoum.

It was with the proceeds from the sale of Height of Fashion that the Queen purchased the famous West Ilsley training

Shirley Heights pictured at Sandringham where he has proved to be a big success.

stables north of Newbury which were then presided over by Nashwan's trainer, Major Dick Hern. His successor is Lord Huntingdon, whose brother-in-law, Ian Balding, trains the remainder of the royal string at Kingsclere.

Racing fortunes tend to run in cycles and the Royal Studs did conspicuously well during the 1950s and 1970s, but less well in the intervening decades. It looks as though the pattern of peaks and troughs is being repeated as Her Majesty achieved her best total in terms of prize money won during 1990.

That season, the four-year-old mare, Starlet, became the Queen's first winner in Germany with a Group 2 victory at

Cambridge Stud

Patrick and Justine Hogan

The 1990 visit of H.M. The Queen to the Cambridge Stud.

It is an honour and a privilege to send greetings and congratulations on this special occasion. Not only do we salute our Queen on Her Majesty's 40th Anniversary but through the New Zealand Thoroughbred Breeders Association, our Patron as well.

1990 was a special year as we were honoured with a Royal visit to Cambridge Stud where Her Majesty The Queen inspected our champion sire Sir Tristram. We were also delighted that the Royal schedule included the opening of the New Zealand Thoroughbred Breeders Association's new headquarters building at Ellerslie Racecourse.

The Cambridge Stud was delighted to be so closely linked to such special occasions. It is with our great respect and affection that we send this anniversary salute with the very best wishes for a long, healthy and happy reign for many years to come.

Patrick and Justine Hogan

Frankfurt. The previous year Starlet's gelded half-brother, Unknown Quantity, won a Grade 1 contest at Arlington Park, Chicago, her first homebred winner in the United States.

Starlet raced in foal to Sharrood, who stands at Highclere Stud owned by the Queen's racing manager, Lord Carnarvon. Furthermore she is by Teenoso, Sharrood's

Big Game and Sun Chariot, winners of four of the substitute classics at Newmarket during 1942, from the National Stud.

It was Carrozza, also leased from the National Stud, but trained by Sir Noel Murless, who provided Her Majesty with a first classic triumph in the 1957 Oaks. Four years earlier, Aureole, a homebred son of Hyperion, finished runner-up in the Derby

The Queen at Newmarket with her trainer Ian Balding and Lord Carnarvon, her racing manager.

erstwhile stud companion there. Henry Carnarvon has been racing manager since 1970 which coincided with the appointment of Michael Oswald as manager of the Royal Studs, the first time there had been two separate departmental heads.

While Michael Oswald manages the Royal Studs and its thoroughbred breeding stock, Lord Carnarvon liaises between the Queen, her trainers and their jockeys. With a background that covers all aspects of the sport, he has a very wide knowledge of breeding and is enormously experienced.

The Queen and Lord Carnarvon (then Lord Porchester), have been close friends since their paths crossed at Fred Darling's Beckhampton stables during the war. At that time, her father, King George VI, leased the celebrated duo of

for the Queen in the year of her coronation.

Aureole, who won the King George VI and Queen Elizabeth Stakes despite a very wayward temperament, spent the duration of his stallion life at Wolferton Stud where he exerted a profound influence. He was champion sire of 1960 and 1961, and is grandsire of Vaguely Noble, another dual champion sire.

The origin of Aureole's distaff family at Sandringham rests with his grandam, Feola. A yearling purchase in 1934, she was placed in the 1000 Guineas and Oaks. As well as Angelola, the dam of Aureole, she had two more distinguished daughters in Hypericum (1000 Guineas), and Above Board (Yorkshire Oaks). One of Above Board's sons, Doutelle, became a noted stallion at Sandringham despite dying young.

The outstanding filly bred by the Queen from the Hypericum line is her granddaughter, Highclere, who became the first ever winner of the 1000 Guineas and Prix de Diane (French Oaks), in 1974. Not only was she named after Lord Carnarvon's home, but she was also conceived there by Queen's Hussar. Sadly this 21-year-old mare died in February whilst foaling in America.

brother to her then principal trainer, Sir Cecil Boyd-Rochfort. The mating of Doutelle with Stroma produced Canisbay. Successful in the Eclipse Stakes, he stood at the Royal Studs before going to Italy where he became a leading sire.

Few winners can have given the Sovereign more satisfaction than Dunferm-

Dunfermline, ridden by Willie Carson, wins The Oaks in 1977, the Queen's Silver Jubilee year.

Highclere produced a good son in Milford, but an even better daughter in Height of Fashion. Both won three Group races — in the Princess of Wales's Stakes, the filly bettered the course record held by her half-brother.

Her Majesty's other two classic winners, Pall Mall and Dunfermline, both owe their origins to sales' bargains. Pall Mall's dam, Malapert, was bought for just 100 guineas as a three-year-old in 1949, while Dunfermline's grandam, Stroma, cost only 1,150 guineas as a yearling in 1956.

Stroma was selected by the Queen entirely upon her own judgement at the old Doncaster sales in a draft from Middleton Park Stud, owned by Harold Boyd-Rochfort,

line, who gained fairytale wins in the Oaks and St. Leger of 1977, her Silver Jubilee year. In the St. Leger, Dunfermline defeated Alleged, who was destined to win the next two runnings of the Prix de l'Arc de Triomphe. Unfortunately she was not a good broodmare, proving difficult to get in foal.

It was at the suggestion of the late Capt. Peter Hastings-Bass, Ian Balding's father-in-law, whom he succeeded at Kingsclere, that the Queen sent a nucleus of mares to board on a semi permanent basis in Kentucky where they could visit some of the outstanding stallions located in the Blue Grass state.

The plan of campaign was instigated in the 1960s resulting in the influential Native Dancer matron, Strip the Willow, and has continued down to the present time. The

Queen has four mares there at present, divided between Will Farish's Lane's End Farm, and Dr. and Mrs. John Chandlers' Mill Ridge Farm.

Dam of Unknown Quantity and Starlet, Pas de Deux, by the Triple Crown hero, Nijinsky, is the most significant dividend from the American connection thus far. Her dam, Example, won the Park Hill Stakes

This is confirmed by Lord Carnarvon. "The Queen takes a great interest in both breeding and racing and would have made an excellent trainer. During the racing season, I probably speak to her two or three times a week on the telephone giving her details of how any of her horses have run or plans regarding any future runners.

Bustino, one of the three stallions at the Royal Studs.

(the fillies' equivalent of the St. Leger) and Prix Jean de Chaudenay. Sadly, Example died foaling Pas de Deux, her solitary offspring, who was reared on a foster mother.

It is well known that the Queen is fascinated by bloodstock breeding which affords her principal relaxation from affairs of state. Extremely knowledgeable about pedigrees and conformation, she is also very keen on the veterinary aspects of the equine world and on all the work that goes on behind the scenes, both in the racing stable and on the stud farm.

"Because of her enormous number of engagements, the Queen is not able to go racing as often as she would like, but she does go to Newmarket when she also takes the opportunity to visit public studs and look at some of the new stallions. She also comes quite frequently to Highclere which enables her to see her yearlings at Polhampton Lodge and to visit West Ilsley and Kingsclere."

The Royal Studs in Norfolk accommodate three stallions. Bustino and Belmez are at Wolferton, and Shirley Heights is at Sandringham, the two studs being three

AN INTERNATIONAL SALUTE . . .

De Beers Industrial Diamond factories and offices throughout the world salute Her Majesty on forty years of responsible, sensitive leadership through some of the most momentous and often difficult times our world has witnessed. The core values of family unity; high moral standards; the education of our youth and the protection of the environment which have characterised Her Majesty's reign are more important now than ever before in an ever-changing world of high technology and challenge which tests democracy and the spirit of free enterprise to the limit.

Long live the Queen!

miles apart. It was thanks to approaches made by Henry Carnarvon to their racing owners that Bustino and Shirley Heights, both syndicated stallions, commenced covering there.

"We were lucky to get Bustino," he recalls. "One day at Newbury races I asked Lady Beaverbrook and her racing manager, Sir Gordon Richards, up to the box to have a glass of champagne. I mentioned that the Queen would like to stand Bustino at Sandringham and she immediately agreed — the very next day Lady Beaverbrook turned down a big offer for her horse from E. P. Taylor, the Canadian breeder of Northern Dancer."

"When Shirley Heights passed the winning post in the Derby, his owner-breeder, the late Lord Halifax, was up in the royal box. I mentioned to the Queen that he might well consider standing this son of Mill Reef at Sandringham and subsequently she bought a number of shares in the horse. Like Bustino, he has proved a very big success for British breeding."

Winner of the St. Leger and Coronation Cup, Bustino was a singularly appropriate horse for the Royal Studs as Doutelle is his maternal grandsire. An eminently successful sire in his own right, Bustino was champion broodmare sire of 1989 thanks to Height of Fashion's brilliant son, Nashwan.

Whereas Bustino and Shirley Heights are established sires, Belmez, winner of the King George VI and Queen Elizabeth Diamond Stakes, retired to stud in 1991, so his first crop are only foals. He remains the property of his owner-breeder, Sheikh Mohammed. Just recently the Queen completed an exchange of animals with this younger brother to Sheikh Hamdan Al Maktoum. In recent times the Royal Studs have produced a surfeit of females. To counteract this, the Queen has swapped a couple of her two-year-old fillies for two colts.

That is not to say that the Queen does not have some promising homebred colts in training. Amongst the three-year-olds at West Ilsley, Lord Carnarvon singles out Top Register, who finished second on his only outing as a juvenile, and Hierarch, an unraced son of Diesis and Highclere.

It is early days to enthuse about two-year-olds, but the Queen's racing manager is very hopeful about Highclere's Blushing Groom colt, Scarlet Tunic, a three-parts brother in

blood to Nashwan. Incidentally two of the most exciting nominations taken by the Royal Studs for the 1992 season are for Pas de Deux to visit Nashwan, and for Starlet to go to Generous, both Derby winners.

To win the Blue Riband remains the Queen's primary objective, but Lord Carnarvon is the first to recognise that breeding is very much a numbers game. With

Ian Balding, one of the Queen's trainers, at Royal Ascot.

a stud of eighteen mares compared to the Arab legions, the odds are stacked against winning as never before. It is ironic that the nearest she should have come to winning the Derby was in the year of her accession.

Sha Tin Racecourse

40th ANNIVERSARY

"The Royal Hong Kong Jockey Club was honoured by the presence of Her Majesty at the inauguration of our Queen Elizabeth II Cup Race on 5 May, 1975, and her subsequent visit to the Sha Tin Racecourse on 22 October, 1986."

"Warmest congratulations on the 40th anniversary of Her Reign as Queen of the United Kingdom and Head of the Commonwealth."

The Royal Hong Kong Jockey Club

Highclere Stud, owned by the Queen's racing manager Lord Carnarvon, after whom one of the Queen's most successful horses was named.

Lord Carnarvon also emphasises that Her Majesty's racing and breeding interests do not have limitless funds at their disposal. "The whole operation is financed entirely out of the Queen's private money. We have to try and make ends meet which is difficult because everything, the well made and the not so well made, all go into training."

Her Majesty the Queen has been a great supporter of the Turf over forty years. To win the Derby may seem a pipe-dream, but then who would have contemplated winning two English classics to commemorate her Silver Jubilee?

PERSONAL MEMORIES

by Godfrey Talbot

For more than fifty years Godfrey Talbot has been writing and broadcasting on the Royal Family and has gained unique insight and experience of the people and personalities that make up the Royal Household. Here he shares some of his experiences.

The diaries I have kept year after year whilst on broadcasting assignments during the Queen's years have been much thumbed as the editorial pieces contained in this publication have been compiled. They have proved useful for factual record of royal occasions, but the personal impressions and the diversions jotted-down at the time have been more evocative on re-reading than all the catalogues of dates. They tell first-hand experiences not in the history books!

Some of the stories, of course, come from way-back: recollections of a young Sovereign 'on the air' during the months of sailing round the globe in that Shaw Savill liner, the *S.S. Gothic*, which was converted into the Royal Yacht before *Britannia* was first brought into service.

One of the very earliest of the Queen's speeches at the microphone during her reign was made on board *Gothic* in the middle of the Pacific Ocean during the first stages of that very long and memorable world tour following the 1953 Coronation. I was the BBC's commentator with the royal party and we were outward bound, Panama Canal behind us and, with calls at Fiji and Tonga just ahead, were making for New Zealand. It was December. Her Majesty was due to make the Sovereign's Christmas Day message soon; and, for once, it was to be spoken away from the homeland (in just about as distant a city as possible) from Auckland in fact, very soon after we reached that city.

One of the official photographs taken at the time of the accession was this classic portrait by Dorothy Wilding.

In those days, broadcasts from overseas really were 'wireless' — not by good-quality land lines and cables and communication satellites. They were simply beamed into the air, and change-able atmospheric conditions often distorted or even eliminated the words before their sounds were received in Britain. So, on this 1953 occasion, lest sun-spots or any other interferences should prevent the royal voice coming clearly from the Antipodes on the Christmas Day, the Queen had agreed to make a stand-by recording of her speech, which would be transmitted from London if 'live from Auckland' proved impossible on December 25.

So there I was, in Her Majesty's lounge aboard the Yacht, my microphone on a table before her and my engineer on the line, as we knew: he was bent over a disc-recorder in the bowels of the ship. I remember that, as the vessel listed gently on the Pacific rollers, tilting the script in front of the speaker, that royal room presented an unusual 'studio' scene. In the four corners stood Prince Philip (listening critically), me (as the cue-to-start signaller), the Queen's Page and the Sergeant Footman (both of whom had discarded their livery and were uniformed in cricket shirts, white shorts and sandals — by pressure of the tropical weather and permission of their employer). All of us, except the Queen herself, were a bit tense. She indeed was amused at everyone else's anxiety, and assured me that she was ready for whatever rehearsals and repeats might be necessary. Calmly and with

For many years now, the Christmas Message — which has become part of a traditional Christmas Day — has of course been broadcast from England, whether Her Majesty has been at Windsor or at Sandringham — to millions of listeners and viewers by radio and by television. It is in fact pre-recorded. Tapes and film (now video tapes) are produced and packaged in advance so that they may be sent world-wide ready for transmission by countries all over the world whose Christmas Day afternoon times (which means 3pm usually) differ from the time in the United Kingdom.

The Queen's speaking of the annual broadcasts is diligent and sincere, though in the early years many people had the impression

V.E. Day, May 1945, crowds cheer as the Royal Family appear on the balcony. Later that day the two Princesses slipped out and joined the throng.

smiles, she made the run-through and the recording without a fluff.

From Fiji next day I flew the discs to London's keeping. In the event, they were not needed. Conditions for the Auckland transmission were excellent and the broadcast was 'live', the Sovereign (gowned for coolness) delivering her Christmas Day greeting on a sultry summer night in the Antipodes.

that Her Majesty was, understandably, a little stiff in manner under the strain of the lights and cameras. But she will never 'act a part' and takes all her tasks so carefully and seriously that sometimes it shows. Yet the fact is that the Queen possesses a marvellous smile, which transforms her whole impression when it comes. Through the years, television producers have striven hard to present to the public the natural ease and enjoyment which are strong

 **Koç**

We, the Koç Group, offer our warm congratulations on the occasion of the 40th Anniversary of the Accession of Her Majesty Queen Elizabeth II.

Over the last four decades we have seen rapid and extraordinary changes in the society in which we live, but Queen Elizabeth II has been a calm and stable presence throughout that time, a constant and well-informed figurehead, steadfast in her dedication and devotion to duty and family. She has been an inspiration to us all.

For many years Turkey has held the British Royal Family in high esteem. It has always been a great pleasure and a privilege to act as host to Royal visitors and we retain particularly warm memories of the State Visit to Turkey in 1971 paid by the Queen and the Duke of Edinburgh. The seven days spent visiting our country are still remembered with great affection by all who saw and met the Royal couple.

The 100 companies and the 40,000 staff of Koç Group join together to take the opportunity to wish a long life and continuing happiness to Her Majesty Queen Elizabeth II, her family and her people.

Rahmi M. Koç
Chairman

features of her character.

In the early years, when the annual messages were spoken from the Queen's own desk, and done 'live' (simultaneously by radio and television in the years 1957 to 1959), one of the moves offered to help Her Majesty to be more relaxed at 3 o'clock on the Christmas Day afternoon was the making of a short and quite informal film, only for the Queen's private viewing, by the then BBC Television announcer Sylvia Peters. It was thought that Sylvia might demonstrate how to speak to a script or to sentences displayed on a screen as though *not* reading the words. A good and well-intentioned notion, but in the Royal Household it was felt that, although the schooling was kindly meant, the film was of little assistance. I think that Sylvia's experienced professionalism — lovely bright person though she quite naturally was — was probably quite daunting!

Since then (in the hands of producers who included Anthony Craxton, Richard Cawston and Sir David Attenborough), the Queen's messages have become more informal and popular. They have sometimes had pre-filmed shots of the Queen at work and at home and with some of the family. Corgi dogs around her have helped too. The royal broadcaster has become accustomed to the matter of reading teleprompters, the word-displaying devices beside the camera lenses. Occasionally a deliberately informal setting has been the Buckingham Palace garden — though things are not automatically easier on home ground: there was one year when an outdoor 'prompter' screen, placed near the Queen as she stood by the edge of the Palace lake during filming, slipped and tilted towards the water so that the displayed words were blurred and jammed. It was a measure of the Queen's ability to cope with the unexpected that she simply smiled and continued calmly to talk, from memory and a stand-by script, betraying no hesitation. By contrast, the faces of the camera crew were a nightmare sight.

I ought not to have been surprised at the Queen's coolness in crisis when (and here I am again remembering that post-Coronation tour of 1953-54) I had the BBC microphone in front of her on board ship as, in the *Gothic*, we were heading into the Indian Ocean and the Queen was ready to make a 'live' radio farewell to Sri Lanka (Ceylon then). I was standing by, waiting to hear a hand-over cue form our reporter on shore in Colombo harbour when, without warning the radio link snapped and we completely lost the shore circuit. I was dependant on the spoken signal which would tell me that the moment had come to introduce the royal voice. But my headphones went dead. Not a sound. What was I to do? I whispered my agonising pre-

Occasionally, the Queen has recorded her Christmas message outdoors.

dicament to Her Majesty, who — the last person in the world to flap — smiled reassuringly at not only me but at the yacht's communications officer and Prince Philip who too were in a state of worried puzzlement at the back of the room. After a silence of a minute or so, it was the Queen who turned to me and said: 'I think it will be all right: this is the time we *should* begin. Pause a moment, then make the announcement so that I can follow your cue'.

Which is what we did. And, as was discovered when communication was restored later, it had all worked perfectly: the Queen was heard just as expected, so much 'on time' that the handing-over commentator on shore didn't know that we never received his signal. The Lord High Admiral — which is one of the Queen's titles — must have 'second-hearing' if not second-sight, I thought.

The years of travel round the world in the train of the Sovereign brought me to speak commentaries into a variety of microphones, not only in parliamentary buildings and banquetting halls but from festival canoes, speeding motorcades and even the backs of state-dressed elephants in Kandy, Kathmandu

guarded frontier post to get a glimpse, across the stark mountains, of a forbidding Communist country before going back down the road to the Jamrud Fort and Peshawar. And I was determined to describe them at this outpost on the road that led west to Kabul.

But all was not well with my recording apparatus. I had to sit in a ditch at the top of the Pass, I remember, tinkering desperately with the recording box slung from my shoulder. The ribbon of tape had become tangled, and the spindles wouldn't turn; and, as I fidgeted with the thing, several other

The Khyber Pass which the Queen and the Duke of Edinburgh visited in 1961.

and Benares. Not every report, therefore, was vouchsafed 'live' to the world (certainly not those being spoken when I fell out of a Nigerian canoe and off the back of an Indian elephant), and indeed many were made into a small tape recorder hugged in my lap.

One description was put on record literally 'by royal permission'. We were in Pakistan for a fortnight during five weeks of State Visits to the Indian sub-continent early in 1961, and on one crisp morning I had gone a little way ahead of Her Majesty and Prince Philip who were driving up the historic Khyber Pass as far as the Afghanistan border. They were going to halt at a viewpoint just short of the heavily

sightseers — English-speaking people who had come up from the Fort — kept halting to chat, saying hello and that they'd heard me on the wireless. I had to say, several times, a hello and a 'Thank-you but please leave me alone because I'm having technical trouble'. When I heard still more footsteps approaching I called, over my shoulder, 'I can't talk to you just now. Must get this damn tape threaded — because *They* may be here at any moment'. This produced gusts of laughter behind my back; and I turned round to find the Queen and the Duke standing over me. They had left the cars a little way down the road, wishing to walk to the viewpoint.

It was characteristic of their customary

interest in how the broadcasts were getting through —— and their thoughtfulness for the tribulations of their itinerant newsman — that they paused beside my trench until I'd got the machine working and myself talking.

The Queen's own voice, of course, has long become a known one because of years of speeches on special occasions. What she says is exemplary in clarity and carefulness. Those critics who lament that the royal deliveries are still unexciting might well be reminded that we have a Sovereign who is very mindful of the British constitution's limitations of what she can say in public: political and personal views are not for airing; and, of all the Royal Family, the Queen never gives an interview. There was, however, just one time when she came near to such a thing — and a happy variant it was for me personally.

The exceptional occasion came in May 1985 when Her Majesty spoke to me about an experience which she described as 'one of the most memorable moments of my life'. It was something that had happened in 1945, and she had never told of it before.

The occasion was the commemoration of the 40th anniversary of the day the main fighting in World War Two ended: V.E. (Victory in Europe) Day. I was helping the BBC to prepare a big radio programme giving personal memories from all sorts of people about what they did and how they celebrated when the longed-for peace was declared. I knew that on that May 8th, night of wild rejoicing in London the Queen (then a 19-year-old Princess Elizabeth in her

During her reign the Queen has become more and more accustomed to the cameras and machinery of broadcasting.

khaki ATS uniform) and her sister Princess Margaret had appeared with her parents, the King and Queen, time after time on the Buckingham Palace balcony — *and* I knew that also she had gone down and for hours mixed with the crowds below, absolutely unrecognised. I thought how splendid it would be if we could get the Monarch to tell the story, and even 'voice it' herself, so that I might use it along with the recollections of her subjects at the time. My colleagues said: 'Not a chance, Godfrey. No use trying.' But I did frame a plea to the Palace, and, to my joy, back came word that the Queen would see me, plus microphone and recording-gear — 'but no cameras'.

When I went into the big house the next Monday I found Her Majesty happy and ready to talk. In her hand were some notes which she had written on Windsor Castle paper during the weekend; and here is how, on record, she described her adventure:

'I realised that my sister and I couldn't see what the crowds were enjoying as they looked up at the balcony. My mother had put her tiara on for the occasion, so we asked my parents if we could go out and see for ourselves. Down in the crowds, we cheered the King and Queen and then walked miles through the streets. Coming back, we stood outside the Palace and shouted 'We want the King! We want the King!' and were successful in seeing my parents on the balcony yet again at midnight — having cheated slightly, because we sent a message into the house to say we were waiting outside'.

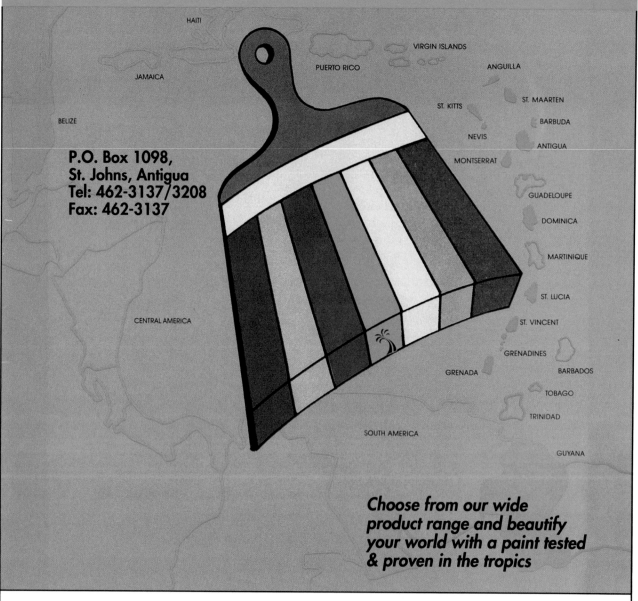

For that unique flashback I was grateful to friends in the Palace who had rightly judged that the public would find special interest and new pleasure in hearing their Sovereign talk about the fun she had, years ago, in that novel adventure (the Queen had also told me how she had been literally lifted off her feet that night by the sheer pressures of the dense crowds, without anybody having the least idea that they were carrying their future Queen along with them on their flag-waving way through streets that had been blacked-out for over five wartime years).

The Private Secretary, Sir William Heseltine, I suspect, as well as Michael Shea who was Press Secretary at the time, had been my helper. One of the bonuses of my job has been the kind and courteous relationships extended by successive Private Secretaries, knowing them as agreeable human beings as well as heavily responsible cogs in the machinery of the monarchy. Their office is the essential channel of communication between Queen and Government. Incisive and meticulous operators, they are also models of politeness and good manners in a world now lacking in such attributes.

Notable examples of the polished Private Secretary tradition during the present Queen's reign have been Martin Charteris (now Lord Charteris of Amisfield) and his predecessor Michael Adeane (the late Lord Adeane). The character and style of each wove indelible threads in the fabric of the decades. Charteris, who efficiently occupied the top position for five invigorating years, 1972 to 1977, is remembered for his infectious zest and unflagging wit. Michael Adeane, a 'natural' for any Court, was a bridge between the Queen's reign and her father's, having been an assistant P.S. to King George VI. He served Her Majesty for nearly twenty years, always recognised and admired as a neat and formal administrator, a tiger for protocol and prerogatives, quiet and scholarly in behaviour, and also delightfully entertaining company.

There is a note in one of my diaries about Sir Michael's skill with words. The note said: '. . . what a little jem of an Adeane whipcrack, so gentle and so effective!'; and it sprang from one of the times I was professionally interested in the personnel of a major ceremony, the annual spectacle of the State Opening of Parliament. We duly broadcast the occasion, but it transpired that Sir Michael had made one of his exemplary understatements in a reminder-of-duty to a Labour Government minister who had a part to play in the ritual procession but didn't want to go. The minister was the late Dick Crossman, then Lord President of the Council, who had asked to be absent from the occasion because he thought it outmoded and pointless. Adeane — most suavely — said to Crossman that, of course, public ceremonies could be as irksome to Her Majesty as they could be to Ministers; but, he went, on '. . . It

A portrait by Prince Andrew to mark the Queen's 60th birthday.

will certainly occur to The Queen to ask herself why you should be excused when she has to go, since you are both officials . . . All you need to do is to write a letter to her . . .'

The Lord President did not write. On the day, he punctually turned up on parade at the Palace of Westminster.

There have been many Westminster occasions in the years since then. More to come, I see, as I turn the pages for *this* year. Busy times with other parliaments too.

But looking back now, reading my own jottings added to the official calendars of royal engagements undertaken, the chronicles get more and more crowded. In almost every December-end I have noted something like 'hectic days, but now for a break . . . hope the Queen will relax in Norfolk'. Those were references to Sandringham of course: the Christmas family gathering and then the first weeks of the New Year, all planned to be spent in residence at that rambling house in the Norfolk countryside. A change, yes, but, for the Queen, there is never such a thing as a complete holiday. 'The boxes', the piles of official paper-work, arrive on her desk every day of every year, wherever she may be.

As 1992 begins, the sheer spread of the royal programmes make a probably unprecedented twelve month-schedule for the by the fact that the Queen herself is to cross the Channel with an unusual impress. Important State tours in both France and Germany are listed, and, during the coming summer, Her Majesty is to visit the Council of Europe in Strasbourg and will deliver an address to the European Parliament.

All this the Queen will be doing as a

The Queen takes her work seriously but can show through a radiant smile the natural ease and enjoyment of her role.

Sovereign — the most tightly-packed set of duties since the Silver Jubilee year of 1977. Commonwealth tours, which started with Australia in February, included a visit to New South Wales for the celebrations of the one hundred and fiftieth anniversary of the foundation of the City of Sydney. Then Canberra, the Federal capital, and on to the State of South Australia.

But, for this year of 1992, and for the first time, Europe looms almost as large as the Commonwealth in the picture ahead — not merely because of the British Government's closer association with the Continent, but sovereign who is far and away Europe's — and indeed the world's — most experienced Head of State (although, as to exact length of office, King Baudouin of Belgium ascended his throne one year before Her Majesty came to hers). Whether her sovereignty will contract or expand in the inevitable European 'togetherness' remains to be seen.

Certainly her forty years of service form a Jewel in the Crown. May it be that the diaries of the Nineties will record that the jewel's coalescent glow has become a guiding light even beyond the southern end of That Tunnel?

A 40th anniversary photograph taken to mark the Queen's Ruby wedding anniversary. Pictured at Windsor Castle the Queen wears the Order of the Garter sash, the Garter Star, the Family Orders of George V and George VI, and the tiara given to her on the occasion of her marriage by Queen Mary.

ACKNOWLEDGEMENTS

Photographs

Cover: Terry O'Neill/Camerapress. **BBC:** 125 (right), 162, 163, 164, 165, 166. **Camera Press:** 7, 19, 25, 26, 29, 30, 31 (right), 35, 38, 39, 45, 47, 49, 51, 52, 53, 58 (left), 61, 64, 74, 83, 85, 87, 88, 109, 119 (bottom), 127, 129, 137, 140, 156, 182 (Cecil Beaton), 191, 200, 223 (Prince Andrew). **Gerry Cranham:** 207, 209, 210, 211, 213, 215. **Crown Estates:** 157, 159, 161. **Duchy of Lancaster:** 155. **Tim Graham:** 9 (left (Lichfield)), 31 (left), 33, 37, 48, 55, 57 (top), 58 (right), 59, 63, 67, 77, 81, 105, 106, 107, 111, 115, 118, 121, 133, 135, 138, 139, 153, 168, 171, 172, 173, 175, 177, 179, 183, 185, 189, 192, 193, 197, 201, 204, 204, 221, 224, 225. **Hulton Picture Collection:** 126 (left), 217. **Hutchinson:** 220. **ICI Chemicals & Polymers Limited:** 101. **Mayotte Magnus/Jorge Lewinski:** 91, 92, 93, 95, 97. **National Portrait Gallery:** 216. **Terry O'Neill:** 84. **Press Association:** 20, 27, 41, 42, 89, 113, 206, 219. **Quadrant (Flight):** 44. **Rex Features:** 65, 70, 71, 73, 79, 117, 119 (top), 126 (right), 169, 199. **© Royal Anniversary Trust:** 15, 17. **Courtesy of The Royal Collection:** 36, 143, 144, 145, 147, 149. **Spectrum:** 131, 205. **Topham:** 9 (right), 21, 23, 57 (bottom), 68, 69, 75, 113, 120, 122, 123, 125 (left), 178, 181, 187, 188, 195.

Editorial: The New Elizabethan Age (page 41) © The Daily Telegraph plc 1992. Elizabeth R (page 162) © Edward Mirzoeff.

Copyright

Publishers Note

In appreciation of the invaluable assistance received in producing this publication Atalink Ltd would like to thank all those companies and individuals whose contributions to the publication have made this tribute possible. In particular, special thanks to Godfrey Talbot for his inestimable assistance and guidance, to Richard Kyle for his inspiration, energy and enthusiasm, to The Netherlands British Chamber of Commerce, Hemmington Scott Publishing Ltd, Kompass Directories — the authority on British industry, The Bankers Almanac, The Longman Group, Economist Publications, Business Week, Tasiemka Archives and The Royal Encyclopedia (Macmillan) edited by Ronald Allison and Sarah Riddell which was an invaluable reference source.